PENGUIN BOOKS

AN UNFINISHED CONVERSATION

Chris Gudgeon is an author, songwriter and musician. He lives in Toronto with his wife, Barbara Stewart, and their black lab, Elvis. Chris is half the brains behind the band The Hounds of Baskerville.

THE LIFE AND MUSIC OF
Stan Rogers

TO: Ron
FR: Rita
Xmas 94'

An Unfinished
Conversation

CHRIS GUDGEON

Penguin Books

PENGUIN BOOKS
Published by the Penguin Group
Penguin Books Canada Ltd, 10 Alcorn Avenue, Toronto, Ontario, Canada M4V 3B2
Penguin Books Ltd, 27 Wrights Lane, London W8 5TZ, England
Penguin Books USA Inc., 375 Hudson Street, New York, New York 10014, U.S.A.
Penguin Books Australia Ltd, Ringwood, Victoria, Australia
Penguin Books (NZ) Ltd, 182-190 Wairau Road, Auckland 10, New Zealand

Penguin Books Ltd, Registered Offices:
Harmondsworth, Middlesex, England

First published in Viking by Penguin Books Canada Limited, 1993

Published in Penguin Books, 1994

1 3 5 7 9 10 8 6 4 2

Copyright © Chris Gudgeon, 1993

Queries regarding radio broadcasting, motion picture, video cassette, television and transla-
tion rights shoud be directed to the Author's representative: The Helen Heller Agency, 126
Sackville Street, Toronto, Ontario, Canada M5A 3E7

Manufactured in Canada

Canadian Cataloguing in Publication Data
Gudgeon, Christopher, 1959 -
An unfinished conversation: the life and music of Stan Rogers

Includes index.
ISBN 0-14-023068-8

1. Rogers, Stan. 2. Folk singers - Canada - Biography. I. Title.

ML420.R65G83 1994   782.42162'0092   C93-093502-0

To my mother, Pat Gudgeon. Without her love
and support, none of this would be possible.

To the passengers and crew
of Flight 797.

Acknowledgments

In the process of writing this book, I interviewed over one hundred people; I'd like to thank all of them for helping me recreate the story of Stan's life and music.

Thanks to several of Stan's aunts and uncles who helped me along the way: June Jarvis, Norman Bushell, Lee Bushell and Prescott Rogers.

Thanks to Stan's various friends and associates: Jim Fleming, Caryl P. Weiss, Mitch Podolak, Bill Howell, Nigel Russell, David Woodhead, Sylvia Tyson, Joe Zizzo and in particular Paul Mills, Stan's friend and producer.

A special thanks to Stan's parents Al and Valerie and to his brother Garnet. I appreciate all of their help with this book.

Most of all, thanks to Ariel Rogers, who not only provided me with valuable information and insight, but with encouragement as well. This book could not have been written without her support and generosity.

There are also some other people I'd like to thank for helping me put the book together: Don MacGillivray, my authority on Maritime culture and history, and, after a few drinks, a bloody good step dancer; my friend and literary agent Daphne Hart of the Helen Heller Agency in Toronto; Greg Stephenson, friend and freelance editor and a damn good writer, who helped me clean up the manuscript; Stephen Osborne for his ongoing support and for his magazine GEIST, which provides Canadian writers and readers with a witty and literate forum for examining our culture; and to all the people at Penguin Books Canada, including Martin Gould and

ACKNOWLEDGMENTS

Sharon Barclay, for their valuable comments on the manuscript, and especially my editor Jackie Kaiser, whose foresight and determination made this book a reality.

Finally, thanks to my wife Barbara Stewart who will never again have to listen to me sing a rousing chorus of "Barrett's Privateers" at two o'clock in the morning.

Foreword

Songwriting is a solitary art.

Once songwriters absorb their early influences, a funny thing often happens: their listening becomes more academic, and they tend to stop looking outside themselves for long periods of time in order to get about the business of writing. This can lead eventually to stagnation, but I have found that whenever I reach this point of introversion, something happens to push me right back out into the middle of things — to make me start listening again.

One of these turning points came in 1974 when I was approached by Paul Mills to host a weekly CBC Radio show called "Touch the Earth." Initially the concept was to do a folk music show, but since my own definition of folk is a rather narrow one, I suggested that we expand the concept and play live and recorded traditional and roots music, along with those contemporary artists whose roots were apparent in their music — a real mouthful, but it turned out to be a fairly sound policy.

Of course, one of the first performers we featured was Stan Rogers. Stan and Paul were pals from way back, but at the time I hadn't even heard of him. Not that this was particularly surprising; I hadn't heard of half the songwriters we had on the show that first year. Five and a half years later, I knew them all.

I took an immediate liking to Stan's music. He had a great bass-baritone voice and an imposing presence. Stan's songs were always interesting; a bit over-traditional for my tastes, but very good nonetheless. That was Stan-the-performer.

My first meeting with Stan-the-person was at a party at Paul's home. Stan had made a fairly pompous speech about the integrity of the artist, and how if you were good enough — even if you only ever sang songs on your own back porch — you would inevitably be discovered and appreciated. I immediately saw red; there was no way I was going to let him get away with that kind of naive pronouncement. So I went for the jugular.

This pretty well summed up our relationship for the next few years. We didn't have the same friends or work in the same places, so we didn't actually see each other that often. I was of a generation of songwriters even earlier than Joni Mitchell and Neil Young, and as an artist who had struggled to establish myself in the United States in order to survive, I did not take kindly to Stan's suggestion that one should write only Canadian songs for a Canadian audience, now that there finally *was* one.

Needless to say, Stan's views changed as his audience broadened and he himself achieved success south of the border. But he never compromised his music. And I must have mellowed a bit myself, because by the end of the now famous Alberta bus tour of 1980, Stan and I were friends.

♪   ♪   ♪

When I heard the news of Stan's death, I was stunned; I simply did not believe it. With some people, it's not exactly that you expect them to die, but that you are somehow not surprised — maybe it's something in the aura or the lifestyle. Stan should not have died in that accident. It just wasn't time. As good as he was, he was getting better still. I realized that what I felt was terrible anger. The grief came later.

Giving my deposition to the two southern airline lawyers — dark-suited, bow-tied, suspendered — was not an experience I'd care to repeat. Their questions were pushing me to sum up a creative life in dollars and cents. I knew it was important to his family, but I resented the hell out of the approach.

"How successful would you say Stan Rogers was?"

(As compared to whom, I wondered?)

"How many concerts a year would you say he did? How many club performances? How many records?"

(No idea.)

"We have a poster here of one of his last shows that puts him last on the bill," they say.

("I think you will find that the names are listed alphabetically," I reply.)

"Would he have become as successful as, say, the Beatles?"

("Stan was not that kind of performer," I answer. "He would have had the kind of long, solid career of, say, Roger Wittaker or Nana Mouskouri, but enhanced by the strength of his songwriting.")

"Did he ever talk to you about how much he was earning?"

(I've finally had enough. "No, no, you don't understand. Canadians don't talk about money, especially when they're doing well. They think it's in bad taste.")

♪   ♪   ♪

The essence of Stan's life, with all its contradictions, is captured in this book. And in the end, it's the contradictions that make Stan Rogers so fascinating to so many people. You can see it in his attitude towards women. Stan Rogers took great delight in his own particular brand of male chauvinism, and yet the two women in his life whom I knew — his mother and his wife — are extraordinarily strong. His persona was tough, but his songs could be tender and poetic.

Those of you who knew Stan will discover in these pages an abundance of memories to rejoice in. Those of you who never had the pleasure during his too-brief life will meet him now, warts and all: Stan-the-performer and Stan-the-man.

Sylvia Tyson

Contents

Introducing...

Stan Rogers, Maritime folk singer.

To many it was as simple as that. Stan, the hearty, jovial sea-farer who hailed from some fishing community on Nova Scotia's eastern shore, was an evocative symbol. To fans around the world, he embodied the popular image of this country: vast and weathered, a wilderness tempered with a touch of British civility, a country of sensible, hard-working, working-class people with middle-class sensibilities.

But behind the straightforward public image — his friends called this image "Maritime Stan" — was a complex man. He wasn't even from the Maritimes. His parents both came from Nova Scotia, but Stan was a Hamilton boy, born and raised. And while Stan spent his career chronicling the struggles of the working class, he never joined their ranks.

Stan could be difficult. While thoughtful and compassionate in song, in life Stan was brash, loud, stubborn and outspoken. He was at times a braggart, insensitive, and often intolerant and ill-tempered. His everyday relationships were complicated and intense, which may explain why he thrived on the clearly defined relationship between artist and audience.

The thing is, Stan Rogers might just be the greatest song-writer Canada has ever produced. He was certainly one of the most influential folk musicians of the past twenty years. He changed the way all of us — not just folk music fans — appreciate traditional music, and how we see and understand our country.

While other artists blast their way into the collective unconscious, Stan quietly slipped in through the back door.

Many of his countrymen have never even heard his name, although his songs are instantly recognizable. "He wrote that?" friends typically ask when I play "Barrett's Privateers" or "Northwest Passage" for them. "I thought that song was a hundred years old!"

I believe that Stan Rogers was an "important artist," but don't let that turn you off. This isn't a stodgy academic biography. Stan packed a lot of living into his thirty-three years; it's only fair that this book strive to be as spirited and entertaining as the man himself. But there are a couple things to know right from the start.

First. This book is a collection of stories. They might be true stories or they might be made up. It's hard to know, and maybe it doesn't matter much anyway. Stan was a man who loved to tell stories. Tall and short. The stories included here have been told to me by people who knew Stan — neighbours, friends, family, fellow folk musicians, fans and blood enemies.

Second, Stan Rogers loved to argue. To him, it was better than drinking coffee. That's what got him going. That's how he related to people, how he connected. Those who never argued with Stan could not count themselves among his friends. He loved to argue and he loved the people with whom he argued.

That's why Stan's sudden death in a fire on board Air Canada Flight 797 stung so many. He was a young man and no one expects a young man to die. Besides, he left too many people in mid-argument. Those who knew him and loved him were still mulling over the things-they-should-have-said-the-last-time and the things-they're-going-to-say-the-next-time. They all knew that Stan never really finished a conversation; he just picked up where he left off.

This is where Stan left off. There are lots of good stories here, and, I hope, an argument or two. I don't think Stan Rogers would have wanted it any other way.

And so, without further ado, Ladies and Gentlemen,
  Stan Rogers . . .

Stories

An unfinished conversation
In a picture of the past
Like the one that I just found of you
Of the many that I had
I remember I saw you laughing
With my camera in my hand
We were minutes from a quarrel
And forever from understanding.

Now, I swear you don't remember why we parted
Just like I cannot remember why we loved
Ain't it funny how the past
Makes the better memories last?
'Cause pain fades away,
It all fades away.

"An Unfinished Conversation (It All Fades Away),"
unreleased.

Overture

But that anchor chain's a fetter
And with it you are tethered to the foam,
And I wouldn't trade your life for one hour of
     home.

> "Lock-keeper," from *From Fresh Water*

Sunday, 29 May 1983. Stan Rogers and his band left the stage without a word. When a show went poorly, there was nothing to say. In part it was their own fault: the band had drunk too much before they went on. In part, it was the sound system. The feedback on stage was incredible and at times they could barely hear themselves. But there was something strange in the air. The instruments picked up on it: the guitar, the bass, the fiddle kept falling out of tune, as weary as the men who played them.

When the Kerrville Folk Festival workers saw Stan coming, they made themselves scarce. It was almost three o'clock in the morning and the last thing they needed was an earful of Stan Rogers.

♪   ♪   ♪

After one month on the road, Kerrville was Stan's last show. He'd been as far afield as Bermuda, then made his way across North America down to Texas. Normally Stan and his band travelled in an old Chevy van. None of them liked to fly and, besides, they could carry more gear in the truck. But, on this leg of the tour, there wasn't a lot of time. Within ten days, they had hit Calgary, Vancouver, Victoria, Seattle, San Francisco and finally Los Angeles, where they played four sold-out shows at McCabe's.

They had taken the plane from Los Angeles that morning and were picked up by a festival volunteer in San Antonio, three hours northeast of Kerrville. Kerrville wasn't the best-paying gig but it was worth the effort. Kerrville had prestige; it was a songwriter's festival and it had launched the careers of some of the best musicians in Texas. The band members were bone tired when they arrived at Kerrville. They were scheduled to go on at ten o'clock, but things just dragged on. The boys started with just one beer at ten o'clock to loosen up, aware that they might be called to the stage at any moment. One beer led to another, and they didn't hit the stage until after one o'clock in the morning.

In folk circles, it was called Stan Rogers's Big Band. They didn't just take the stage; they took it over. At six foot four and 235 pounds, Stan was the smallest of the bunch. Garnet Rogers — Stan's accompanist, on-stage foil and younger brother — and bass player Jim Morison completed the line-up. They were three superb musicians with a presence unlike anything folk fans had seen before. The band marched onto the stage that night and launched into the *a cappella* ballad "Northwest Passage" and something clicked.

> Ah, for just one time, I would take the
>   Northwest Passage
> To find the hand of Franklin reaching for
>   the Beaufort Sea
> Tracing one warm line through a land so
>   wild and savage
> And make a Northwest Passage to the sea.

Al Simmons watched Stan's show from backstage. Al was a comedian and musician from Winnipeg who, along with Stan and singer Connie Kaldor, made up the Canadian contingent at the festival. Al had met Stan before, but this was the first time he'd seen Stan in concert.

"Stan later said it was the worst show he'd done in years," Al remembers. "But I was absolutely blown away, and they had the audience absolutely hypnotized. I'd never seen anything like it before. When he sang and when he performed, the power coming off the stage was incredible."

Stan Rogers was the kind of man who stood out in a crowd, even in a crowd like this, full of long, tall Texans. He was a giant man, already bald at thirty-three, with a thick beard and a slight moustache. He had a vaguely scholarly look, a little like a half-crazed history professor. But it wasn't just his physical attributes that caught people's attention. Stan had presence, energy. Musicians called him the "Mount St. Helens of folk music," poking fun at the way steam rose off Stan's bald head when he performed, but also a backhanded tribute to a man who was both explosive and powerful.

♪   ♪   ♪

Stan Rogers was a man of vision and his kind were in short supply in the early 1980s. The Canadian economy had been declining steadily as bankruptcies, unemployment and interest rates all reached record highs, while the political climate was unstable. In barely five years, Canada would have four different prime ministers. Pierre Trudeau — who, twelve years earlier, had embodied a new sense of Canadian identity — now played out his last days as a transitional figure, and an unattractive one at that. It was the era of the "patriated constitution" and "six-and-five restraint"; Trudeau was conceited, sour, gaunt. This was what Canada had become.

Maybe that's why Stan Rogers stood out. At a time when every Canadian was looking for answers, Stan seemed sure of himself and confident about his future. He'd built an international reputation in folk music circles, counting among his many fans such legends as Tom Paxton, Pete Seeger, Sylvia Tyson, and Peter Yarrow of Peter, Paul and Mary fame, who once called Stan "the best young songwriter alive today."

This recognition meant that, for the first time in his life, Stan had some financial stability. He commanded top dollar in many concert halls throughout North America, and the sales of his four independently released records were building steadily. In 1981, he sold fewer than 13,000 albums. The following year, he sold more than 16,000, and only halfway through 1983 Stan had surpassed the previous year's total. Not bad for a record company that operated out of his mother's dining room.

Still, Stan was struggling for recognition in his homeland. Canadians are notoriously fickle, always the last to acknowledge homegrown talent. Talent, especially an obvious talent like Stan's, is considered somehow impolite. To become a success in Canada, Stan often joked, you have two choices: you can either move to the States or you can die.

♪   ♪   ♪

At the end of the set, the Kerrville crowd demanded an encore. Stan obliged with "The Mary Ellen Carter," his most famous song. The story was simple: some sailors salvage a sunken boat. The song paid tribute to those who go against the grain and still find success — people just like Stan Rogers. And as the band rolled into the final chorus, the audience was on its feet, singing along.

> Rise again, rise again — though your
>   heart it be broken
> And life about to end
> No matter what you've lost, be it a home,
>   a love, a friend
> Like the *Mary Ellen Carter*, rise again.

As the house lights went on, there was a wave of applause and a disappointed buzz as the audience realized the show they hoped would never end was now, in fact, complete. That was the thing about audiences: the more Stan gave them, the more they wanted.

White Squall

But I told that kid a hundred times "Don't take
    the Lakes for granted.
They go from calm to a hundred knots so fast they
    seem enchanted."
But tonight some red-eyed Wiarton girl lies staring
    at the wall,
And her lover's gone into a white squall.
                   "White Squall," from *From Fresh Water*

Stan Rogers was out of breath as he took his seat on Air Canada Flight 797. He'd just made his connecting flight and had run from one end of the Dallas airport to the other. Stan was on his way home from Kerrville to Dundas, a small town at the western edge of Hamilton, Ontario. One night's rest at home, then another show the next day at the Fiddler's Green Folk Club in Toronto.

Stan was cursing Air Canada for the benefit of anyone who'd listen. He'd never been a fan of the national airline, which seemed to make a habit of crushing his guitars. Stan was in a cantankerous mood, in any case, suffering from the effects of too much travel and too little sleep.

It was a sultry, calm evening in Dallas, more summer than spring. As the pilot warmed up the engine on the runway, some of the passengers skimmed through the Canadian papers for news of home. There was a lot of speculation about the upcoming Progressive Conservative leadership convention. The smart money was on incumbent Joe Clark, although Newfoundland's John Crosbie was expected to make a good showing. Few pundits gave a relative unknown from Quebec, Brian Mulroney, much of a chance.

At 4:25 central daylight time, Flight 797 took off with forty-one passengers — less than half capacity — and five crew. Its final destination was Montreal, with a brief stop in Toronto.

By seven o'clock that evening, halfway through the five-hour flight to Toronto, many of the passengers were drifting off to sleep. Senior Flight Attendant Sergio Bennetti had just brought the captain dinner when a passenger reported smoke coming from one of the washrooms. Bennetti's first thought was that someone had thrown a cigarette into the trash bin. Since the bins are mounted in fire-resistant casing, this kind of problem would be easy to contain. But when Bennetti opened the washroom door, he didn't see any flames. Instead, black smoke curled out of the seams of the back wall panel above the sink. He flooded the bathroom with foam from the fire extinguisher, closed the door and returned to the cockpit.

♪   ♪   ♪

No one on board could possibly have known the danger they were in. An electrical fire had been burning for fifteen minutes before the first signs of smoke were detected. The flames had already melted the wires on the flush pump, causing the breakers to trip, and by the time the first smoke was detected the fire had spread through the ceiling.

Once he was aware that there was a problem, Captain Donald Cameron quickly decided what to do. At exactly 7:08, he radioed to anyone who could hear.

"Mayday," he said. "Mayday! Mayday! . . . We're going down. We have a fire."

In the cabin, the flight attendants were moving the passengers forward, away from the smoke. Stan Rogers moved forward with the rest of them. As he passed the flight attendant,

she handed him a wet towel to put over his nose and mouth —
a makeshift mask to filter the smoke and fumes.

The emergency descent to the Cincinnati airport lasted
eight minutes. By the time the plane broke through the
clouds, chunks of plastic were falling on the passangers as
the ceiling melted away. One of the survivors told me that
the smoke was so thick, he couldn't see his hand in front
of his face. And yet there was reportedly no panic; the passengers quietly prepared for what was bound to be a rough
landing.

By the time Cameron made his final approach, the cockpit was so full of smoke he had to crouch to see the runway.
As soon as the jet touched down, he slammed on the brakes.
Like everything else, the anti-skid system was out; the four
main tires blew on landing.

Cameron stuck his head out the window and gasped for
air. His first officer Claude Ouimet tried to exit through the
cabin, but was pushed back by the smoke and had to escape
through the cockpit window. When he saw Cameron unconscious in his chair, Ouimet alerted a fireman who blasted the
captain with water. It was enough to rouse Cameron and he
too squeezed through the cockpit window, dropping fifteen
feet to the tarmac.

Inside the cabin, there was no time for organized evacuation. Bennetti sent an ailing passenger down the slide, then
called out to anyone who could hear, although he could barely
draw enough air to speak. He waited at the doorway, until the
heat became too intense.

No one on board Flight 797 saw flames during the emergency descent, but as the plane made its final approach, wit-
nesses on the ground saw flames spew from two holes on top
of the fuselage. Thirteen firefighters were at the ready. They
flooded the top of the plane with foam and sprayed the ground
beneath it to protect against a fuel leak. Two firefighters
attempted to enter the plane from the middle emergency exit.
But, just as they were about to go inside, all hell broke loose.
Barely one minute after the plane had landed, the cabin
exploded into flames.

The end came quickly; the worst was over in seconds. Twenty-three people died in the flames. Eighteen passengers and the entire five-member crew survived.

♪   ♪   ♪

At her home in Dundas, Ontario, Stan Rogers's wife, Ariel, watched the news in horror. There was Flight 797, flames twisting through two giant holes in the roof, while a grim reporter speculated on the number of dead. Ariel tried to get through to Air Canada's office in Toronto, but all they would do was confirm that Stan had been on the flight. They offered no further information.

Ariel was still watching the TV news at four o'clock in morning, when she heard a knock at the door. She opened the door. It was a pair of plain-clothes policemen, who had come to confirm what she already knew in her heart.

History

Well, the track of my beginnings
Has been buried 'neath the years
For a dozen generations,
We have toiled the land here.
                    "Pocketful Of Gold," unreleased

S tan Rogers, dead at thirty-three, an age when most artists are just establishing their careers. Suddenly the country, the world, was taking stock of his legacy. Very quickly, everyone realized that Stan's strongest characteristic was his profound sense of history. The history of the music he loved, the history of his country, the history of his family, the personal histories of people he met along the way — Stan was fascinated with it all.

Stan Rogers had a rich family history of his own. According to legend, the paterfamilias of the Rogers clan was John the Martyr, the first Protestant executed during the reign of Bloody Queen Mary in the sixteenth century. James Rogers, thought to be the martyr's grandson, immigrated to New England in 1635 and became a wealthy plantation owner.

A tradition of religious dissent followed the Rogers family to the New World. James's son John was a notorious religious radical who formed his own breakaway church in 1674. It was a political act, a defiance of the state-supported Congregationalist Church. Even so, with discretion, John and his followers might have continued with little trouble —

religious dissent was a popular recreational activity in pre-
baseball America. But true to his family name, John Rogers
was conspicuous and provocative. He encouraged his congre-
gation to defy the state, and he took great delight in disrupt-
ing Congregationalist Church services. Stan apparently came
by his combative nature honestly.

Stan's Maritime connection dates back to 1760, when
Rolen Rogers, old John's great-nephew, moved to Horton
Township, on and around the Gaspereaux Mountain in Nova
Scotia. There were practical reasons for the move: land was
growing scarce in Connecticut, while Nova Scotia was largely
unsettled. And the Rogerenes, as old John's followers called
themselves, were becoming more disruptive and were often
publically flogged or tarred and feathered for their actions.
Rolen Rogers didn't relish the role of human target; he
wanted to get while the getting was good.

♪   ♪   ♪

Stan's Nova Scotia roots were neither Scottish nor particularly Maritime, but remarkable nonetheless. His paternal
grandfather and namesake was born in Stellarton, Nova Scotia, on February 26, 1889. Stanley Edward Rogers was a lum-
berman, who in 1934 moved to Pictou County and bought a
large farm with a water mill. Stanley was a remarkable man.
He served overseas in both World Wars. He was almost fifty
when World War II broke out and he had to lie about his age
to enlist. He was gentle and industrious, and built a prosper-
ous business with the help of his wife Jaunita Mae — a not-
too-distant cousin of Sir Charles Tupper, a Father of
Confederation — and their eight children.

Stan's Uncle Prescott, Stanley and Jaunita's son, has
fond memories of childhood on the Pictou farm. "We just
thought of ourselves as a typical country family. We did the
usual things. We often had a singsong around the piano on a
weekend. Sometimes we sang hymns, but our music wasn't
restricted to hymns because we sang a lot of the songs popular at the time. Mother played the piano, as did my two sisters.

My oldest brother Emerson was something of a fiddle player. And if we were going to have a little dance music, Dad would get out the mouth organ."

♪   ♪   ♪

Stan's mother Valerie Bushell grew up just outside of Canso, Nova Scotia, in a place called Hazel Hill. The locals say that the area is the most easterly point on the continent, "as close as you can get to Ireland without getting your feet wet." Stan liked to claim that this town might just have been the site of one of the oldest European settlements in the New World. There was evidence, Stan said, that Portuguese fishermen lived in the area before Columbus's era.

Canso is one of the most beautiful spots on the coast. It is off the beaten tourist track, and isn't overshadowed by man-ufactured charm. Standing at the shore, looking across the Chedabucto Bay, you can see Cape Breton rise in the distance. There's little wonder why Stan was drawn to this place all his life.

Valerie's father arrived in Canso a few years after World War I. Sidney Bushell worked as a telegraph operator for the Commercial Cable Company, owners of the transatlantic communication cable that linked North America with the Old World. Sidney was originally from Tunbridge Wells, Kent, England and had spent some time working for the cable company in South America. He was also something of an amateur writer who'd had several of his poems published. One was "Yeastcake Jones," which Stan later set to music and recorded on his 1983 album *For The Family*.

Sidney married Letitia Mary Narraway Hart soon after arriving in Canso. She was from a prominent local family of United Empire Loyalist stock. Her mother was one of the Hal-ifax Smiths, well-to-do merchants who considered them-selves upper crust.

Stan characterized his grandfather as a "poor telegraph operator," but this is misleading. In an area of the country where unemployment was always high, Sidney enjoyed steady work, and, although there were twelve children, the family was comfortable. The Commercial Cable Company had its own clubhouse, tennis courts (proper "whites" were the only acceptable attire), ballroom, boats on the lake — all accessible to employees only. Even the company houses were better than average. They had running water and plumbing, while the rest of the community made do with wells and outhouses.

Valerie Bushell was in her teens in 1946 when she moved from Hazel Hill to find work. She wound up in the town of Amherst on the New Brunswick border. There, she went to business school, worked in a jewelry store, and in the fall she met a young man named Nathan Allison "Al" Rogers, fresh from his stint in the Royal Canadian Air Force. They were engaged a year later, married in July 1948, and moved to Hamilton shortly thereafter to find work. On November 29, 1949, their first son was born and duly christened Stanley Allison Rogers.

Prodigy

On the ridge above Acadia's town to the valley
    down below
The evening falls upon the families listening to the
    radio
And watching the apples grow.
    "Watching The Apples Grow," from *Fogarty's Cove*

This is Stan Rogers's first memory: sitting in his grandmother's kitchen in Hazel Hill, Nova Scotia, in his hand a slice of still-warm bread lathered in peanut butter. The room is hot, filled with the loamy heat of the wood stove and the smells of the kitchen — birchwood burning, bread baking, a giant and perpetual pot of stew. Around him sit his mother and father and grandparents and various aunts and guitar-playing uncles, everyone singing and laughing. In years to come, Stan would recognize the individual songs — by Hank Williams, Jimmie Rodgers and Nova Scotia boys Hank Snow and Wilf Carter — but for now the sounds blend together and that is enough. Other children had fairy tales; Stan had country and western.

BUSHELL BROWN BREAD

To understand the stuff that came out of Stan Rogers's mouth, it helps to know what went into it. Bushell Brown Bread, from his grandmother's recipe, was a lifelong favourite

of Stan. You don't have to allow this bread time to rise. If you
pan the dough right after the first kneading, it makes a deli-
cious dense bread. It's perfect for busy households — which
makes sense when you think of Mrs. Nita Bushell and her
twelve children.

8 cups white flour
8 cups whole wheat flour
3 – 4 tablespoons shortening
1 cup white sugar
4 – 5 tablespoons salt
1 cup molasses
2 – 3 cups lukewarm water
2 envelopes dry yeast

(1) Proof yeast in 1 cup lukewarm water.
    Cut shortening into dry ingredients.
(2) Make a well in the flour mixture. Add
    yeast and molasses.
(3) Add water a little at a time, until
    dough feels pliable.
(4) Pan immediately for dense bread. For
    lighter bread, raise until dough dou-
    bles in size. Then pan.
(5) Bake slowly at 315° F for 1 hour.

Young Stan was by all accounts cheerful and precocious,
and from the start he had an affinity to music. According to
his family, he could sing almost as soon as he could talk. On
visits to Hazel Hill, Stan impressed his grandfather with his
perfect pitch and uncanny ability to improvise.

Stan's parents recognized and encouraged his musical
talent. Valerie, in particular, had refined tastes and made sure
that both her boys were exposed to the classics of music and
literature.

Stan got his first guitar when he was five. It was hand-built by Stan's Uncle Lee Bushell. The boy had hounded his uncle for months, until finally the guitar appeared. As an adult, Stan remembered the "depression-model" Bushell guitar fondly in the winter 1983 issue of the folk magazine *Come For To Sing*:

> The frets are cut from brass welding rods, the nut and saddle were carved from an old toothbrush, the bridge pins are brass beads, and the top, back, sides, neck, fretboard and strap pin were all hand-cut from hardwood birch.
>
> It weighs nearly twenty pounds, has a tone vaguely resembling that of a smallbody Martin. . . . I still play it often, keep it near me in my living room, and will never, ever part with it.

Not long after getting the guitar, Stan made another important discovery. He found that if he took his toy ukulele around to the neighbours and sang a little song, something magical happened. People gave him money — a couple of pennies, maybe, the odd nickel, and every once in a while a shiny, silver dime.

This first crack at a musical career didn't last long. Stan's mom was not happy to hear that Stanley was going to the neighbours for money and his public performances came to a sudden end. He did practise at home, and Garnet remembers how the two of them would sing themselves to sleep each night — Stan instructing his brother, who was six years younger, on the fine points of two-part harmony — listening to country music on a giant RCA Victor tube radio.

♪   ♪   ♪

"Pumpkin head . . ."

The voice trailed off in the singsong refrain of a school-yard taunt. The fat kid in the duffle coat stood silent, this time determined not to let his anger show. But his eyes welled with tears of frustration. These kids were relentless. Day in, day out, they would pick on Stan. It didn't take much, just a couple words, and Stan would lose it.

It's not hard to understand why the kids picked on Stan. He was a smart kid, the kind, his mother says, who liked to use big words nobody else understood. But smart was not always a smart thing to be in a rural Ontario schoolyard in 1960.

At eleven, Stan was big for his age. He'd never been well-coordinated. He shied away from sports, except for mud football, and despite his size he was strangely passive when things got rough. He wouldn't fight back.

Stan did have some friends though. Neighbour Dave Murray was one of his closest. Murray recalls that Stan was mouthy, argumentative and a first-class bullshitter even then. But he also saw another side of Stan.

"We built tunnels in the hay in the old barn behind my house," Murray recalls. "Me and Stan and a couple of other kids from the neighborhood, we'd play for days."

The old barn was, of course, forbidden territory to the boys. Many of the boards were loose or rotten, and there was always the danger that the floor could collapse. It was the perfect place for an eleven-year-old: it had an element of peril and offered a sense of complete seclusion.

"We'd smoke cigarettes in the hay bale tunnels. Can you imagine that? Here we were under twelve feet of hay, in a little compartment we'd made, maybe four feet by six feet, smoking cigarettes, lighting little fires in the hay. And we'd talk to each other, about our hopes, our dreams, our fantasies. And Stan was right there with us. He wasn't trying to show off or be the centre of attention. He was just being himself and letting his true thoughts come out."

Around such friends as Dave Murray, Stan did not seem unusually musical. He would sing on Friday nights with the rest of the gang, as they walked the gravel roads near Stan's home in Tapley Town. Out with the guys, Stan was best known for his volume, rather than his pitch or harmonies. They'd sing the popular songs of the day: "Lollypop," "Wake Up Little Susie," "Leader Of The Pack."

Those were faceless days for pop music. Rock 'n' roll, the white man's rhythm 'n' blues, had flowered in the mid-fifties, and by 1962 it was dead. Elvis was six years past his prime, and flat pop with a tempered backbeat — the music of the Johnnies and Frankies and Bobbies — ruled the radio charts. But popular music was about to change, and when it did, Stan's life changed as well.

Folk Boom

We live in fear of no one to love us
Of feeling like an empty hole
No kind heart or strengthening hand
To light the dark and seeking soul.

"Matter Of Heart," unreleased

There are probably as many definitions of folk music as there are folk fans. Historically, and to purists and academics, it means something quite specific — traditional music, played on traditional instruments, passed on from generation to generation with little variation. But today, most people use "folk" in a much more general sense to refer to popular acoustic-based music, often with an emphasis on introspective or political lyrics. The term can be used in a positive sense to distance a favourite artist from mainstream commercial pop ("After all these years, Dylan remains essentially a folk artist . . . ") or in a negative sense ("Bob Dylan? He's just a tired old folkie . . . ").

In Canada, a large body of "pure folk" music has been preserved, thanks to scholars like Kenneth Peacock, Roy MacKenzie, and Helen Creighton who alone collected more than four thousand folk songs in the Maritimes. Since the fifties, Edith Fowke, a scholar and broadcaster, and her frequent collaborator, the singer Alan Mills, have brought traditional Canadian folk songs to millions through their work in radio and on records.

Those who maintain the strict definition of folk music are often maligned by others within the folk community. Stan himself called them "folk nazis." But the purists have a good point. Without clear boundaries, the term becomes almost meaningless. When you get right down to it, there's little difference between what most people consider folk music and pop music in general; folk music has always been a popular and populist medium, while most of the popular music of this century was based on two folk forms, country and the blues.

This more general meaning of "folk" arose in the 1960s as a result of a revival movement known as the "folk boom." The roots of this revival go back to 1950 when the Weavers' reworking of a traditional song, "Good Night Irene" hit Number One on the pop charts, stayed there for thirteen weeks and sold over two million records. Led by Pete Seeger — one of folk music's most influential figures — the Weavers continued to enjoy success, charting ten hits in two years. But in the mid-fifties the notorious House Committee on Un-American Activities branded members of the band "communists," a blow to both the band — radio wouldn't touch them for years — and to folk music in general.

As the sixties approached, most of the music on commercial radio was pretty bland, and audiences were ready for something new. Along came the Kingston Trio, who sang traditional folk songs. With their conservative haircuts and freshmen good looks they appeared the antithesis of communist agitators. From 1960 to 1962, the Trio recorded six platinum albums and a host of top ten singles.

The success of the Kingston Trio kicked off the so-called "folk boom." Peter, Paul and Mary had a huge hit with "If I Had A Hammer" — co-written by Pete Seeger and fellow Weaver Lee Hays — which gave voice to a growing mood of political and social discontent. Today, people often use "folk boom" as a generic term, but it really refers to a specific period — from the Kingston Trio's first hit, "Tom Dooley," in 1958 to the British Invasion in 1964 — during which like-minded performers who sang contemporary versions of folk songs or wrote their own songs in a traditional style were a dominant commercial force in American music.

♪   ♪   ♪

At the forefront of the folk boom was the Canadian duo of Ian and Sylvia Tyson. Sylvia — who would later play a role in Stan Rogers's career — was born in Chatham, Ontario, in 1940. In the late fifties she teamed up with Ian Tyson, a one-time logger and rodeo rider, originally from British Columbia. The two sang in folk clubs around southern Ontario and eventually made their way to New York where Albert Grossman, who managed the likes of Bob Dylan and Peter, Paul and Mary, saw the duo and signed them up.

Soon, Ian and Sylvia had a contract with Vanguard Records. They recorded half a dozen albums for this company — all of them reaching Billboard's pop charts — and had a number of hit singles including Ian's "Four Strong Winds" and Sylvia's "You Were On My Mind," a Top Five single in 1965 for The We Five.

In 1961, Stan Rogers wasn't worried about issues of definition. For an intelligent, romantic outsider like Stan Rogers, folk music was the perfect form of expression. It offered a sense of community — folk singers encouraged their audience to "sing along" — and appealed to his sense of history. It also proved that intelligence and compassion had a place in popular music. And best of all, it was portable: all you needed was a guitar, a good strong voice, and a love of the spotlight, three things Stan could count among his assets.

Saving Grace

And every kid over the boards listens for
    the sound;
The roar of the crowd is their ticket for
    finally leaving this town.

          "Flying," from *From Fresh Water*

More and more, music became Stan's saving grace. In his brother Garnet's words, music "took the place of a normal adolescence." It gave Stan a new role: the troubadour. When he showed up at a party with his guitar, people were happy to see him. The odd girl — Stan would probably say very odd — might even park herself beside him for the evening.

In his early teens, Stan experimented with rock. He sang and played bass in several bands with names like "Predator" and "Stanley and the Living Stones." But despite his technical proficiency, Stan was not at ease with rock. He had the temperament, he liked to show off and take centre stage, but he wasn't comfortable with the music. And he certainly never looked like a rock star. He tried, but with his heavy black glasses and fluffy pompadour, he wound up looking like a Cro-Magnon Buddy Holly.

By now, Stan was developing a network of musical friends. Though he remained something of an outcast at high school — Stan would later refer to his teenaged self as a "geek" — he fell in with people who shared his love of song. Stan's closest friend at that time was Bill Jurgenson, a schoolmate at Saltfleet

High. Jurgenson recalls that while Stan may have flirted with rock, his real love was folk. He had an innate feel for the music.

"I'd bought an album, one of those how-to-play-guitar things," Jurgenson says. "I managed to pick up a couple finger-picking styles and passed them on to Stan. He just took them and went with them. He was so damn good, and so quick to pick up this stuff."

In 1963, at the ripe old age of fourteen, Stan started playing at coffee houses in Hamilton. His first solo show was at a place called the Ebony Knight, run by painter Bill Powell. He played for two hours and his pay wasn't exactly scale: five bucks and a bottle of cheap wine. Stan's set included familiar folk songs of the day: a couple by Dylan, some traditional tunes like "Black Girl," "Tom Dooley" and "Kum Ba Ya" and an occasional Hank Williams country stomp. Soon, Stan was including an original song or two, although few of these early songs survive.

As Stan began to play more solo concerts, Bill Jurgenson took on the job of manager. Bill, who was a few years older than Stan, would drive Stan to gigs and keep him out of trouble. Stan had always taken his own opinion very seriously, but now there was a new dimension to contend with. At fifteen, Stan sprouted up by a foot: he was his full adult height and quickly learned to use his size to intimidate. His first priority was to settle a few old scores in the old neighbourhood.

Stan's finest moment might just have been the night he and Bill Jurgenson stopped at a bar called the Plantation House. "The waiter asked us for our ID," Bill recalls. "I pulled mine out, and Stan patted his pockets, then told the waiter that he forgot his wallet. The waiter was persistent. The next thing I knew, Stan stood up, pounded his fists on the table and looked down on the waiter. 'Jesus, man, what do I got to do? Bring my fifteen-year-old son in here?'"

The ploy worked. The waiter apologized profusely and promptly brought them some beer. The two had a good laugh as they sipped their beers. Stan had really meant it as a joke, but was also coming to realize that his size and forceful personality had certain advantages.

The Hobbits

I've been sitting here crying since long before the
    day began
With my pockets full of nothing but broken dreams
And my head in my empty hands.
                     "Second Effort," from *Turnaround*

By 1967, Stan had a reputation as one of the brightest young performers on the Hamilton coffee house circuit. His chief competition came from another teenager, Nigel Russell, who specialized in bluegrass guitar. The two were aware of each other, but did not meet until they shared billing at a café called The Wrong Side in 1967. Also on the bill was a fifteen-year-old singer making her professional debut, Terri Olenick.

A photographer from the local paper thought it would make a cute picture if the three performers pretended to play something together. Stan feigned reluctance at first, pretending to be shy. But then he joined the other two, unable to pass up an opportunity to get his picture in the paper. While the camera clicked, they improvised a song. It didn't sound half bad. As a matter of fact, it sounded damn good. And so, the Hobbits were born.

The name came from the Tolkien book, a favourite of Stan's. He had read the entire *Lord of The Rings* trilogy in a matter of days when he was seventeen. The name was

supposed to reflect the personality of the bandmates, in
Terri Olenick's words, "roly-poly, playful, funny hobbits."
At the time, Stan himself looked like an overgrown hobbit.
He had a thin beard which he trimmed often. And although
he was already balding on top, the hair on the sides was
fairly long, with an unkempt look. Because of his size, his
mother made a lot of his clothes and he designed them in a
somewhat medieval fashion with lots of tunics and buckles
and fringe.

The Hobbits marked the first time Stan worked in a trio,
the format he came to favour during his career. Stan and Nigel
played guitars; Stan and Terri shared vocals. They played a
typical folk repertoire, with an emphasis on songs by such
Canadian songwriters as Gordon Lightfoot, Joni Mitchell and
Leonard Cohen.

When the Hobbits started playing together, Nigel was a
student at Trent University in Peterborough, about one hundred miles northeast of Toronto. Stan had tried McMaster
University in Hamilton a year earlier, but his studies were
sidetracked by more serious pursuits: girls and beer. By 1969,
he moved in with Russell in a house dubbed "Little Red" in
honour of The Band's Woodstock home "Big Pink."

This was the most tumultuous period of Stan's life. He
was unclear about his life's direction, a situation that wasn't
helped by a couple of heartbreaking love affairs. Meanwhile,
Nigel Russell recalls, Stan's flirtation with the music business
was creating some tension in his family. His parents had sup-
ported Stan's musical interest from the start. But being practical Maritimers, they hoped that he would choose a more
secure vocation than folk music.

The pressures of growing up were taking their toll. As
Russell saw it, Stan was a walking contradiction: from the outside he appeared strong and confident, but, like any artist, he
had his vulnerable side.

"To look at him you'd think: 'Here's a tough-assed son-
of-a-gun who's been down the road.' Nothing could be further
from the truth. Stan was rather naive; this is at the root of his
songwriting. His lack of experience freed him to go into his

mind and romanticize. He made legends out of stuff that was actually mundane."

Stan seemed constantly at odds with himself. He shielded himself from the kind of rejection that he had known in the playground, but more than anything, he wanted to share himself. He wanted others to recognize his gifts and take them seriously. He would try so hard to express himself that he became nearly inarticulate. This made his music more important than ever to him. It was his saving grace, arrived at only after hours of painstaking rehearsal with attention to the very smallest detail. Performance was not a spontaneous celebration, but a well-earned victory.

Nowhere was Stan's difficulty more evident than in his on-stage patter. In those unrehearsed moments between songs, when Stan had to share himself with the audience, he rarely knew where to begin and, rarer still, when to stop. A review in a London student newspaper tells the story. After praising Stan's rich and resonant voice, the reviewers take exception to his patter:

> Rogers came close to torpedoing the whole affair with his inane babbling. His between-songs chatter might well have built up the rapport he so obviously wanted — if he hadn't been so blatantly self-conscious.

There were uncomfortable moments, true, but there was also a payoff for Stan. He lived for those moments when his singing and playing would enrapture the audience and carry them away. He worked harder and harder at perfecting his performance skills. By the end of 1969, the Hobbits had broken up, but Stan and Nigel continued to play together. Over the next year, Stan took another stab at university, this time joining Nigel at Trent. But his loyalty to the halls of

higher learning was not strong. The songs were coming easier now, and sooner or later he'd have to make up his mind.
Would he follow his heart and become a professional musician or would he find a more conventional career? The
problem would soon take care of itself.

RCA

Way down in the ocean, under the shining sea
The fishes' world is in commotion,
And it's because of me
They think the price of breathing
Is more than I can afford
But I'm living high and doing fine
Without visible means of support.

"Fishes," unreleased

The year was 1970 and suddenly home-grown music was breaking onto the American pop charts. The "Canadian Invasion" was led by the Guess Who, a quartet from Winnipeg which had five U.S. hits that year, including the number one two-sided single "American Woman/No Sugar Tonight." Anne Murray also made the top ten with "Snowbird," and there was a handful of one-off singles like Mashmakhan's stunning "As Years Go By" and the Original Caste's enduring pop parable "One Tin Soldier."

The year also saw a change in the rules that governed Canadian radio. The new rules, designed to encourage radio stations to play more Canadian songs, were simple: thirty percent of the songs played by a station had to fit the special guidelines defined by the MAPLe system. A record got one point for each part of the MAPLe — Music, Artist, Production and Lyrics — that was Canadian. In the early days, one out of four was all that was needed to qualify, so that any song written, performed or produced by a Canadian was eligible. (Canadian content rules are still in effect, although these days a record needs two points to qualify.)

In 1970, the Cancon rules were affecting the kinds of acts record companies signed. Virtually all Canadian record companies were American subsidiaries, which in practice meant two things: the companies weren't very committed to Canadian music, and they didn't expect to make a lot of money from it. The parent companies were reluctant to release Canadian records in the United States, and if a Canadian act met with success, they were quickly signed to the U.S. parent company.

Barry Keane — best-known as Gordon Lightfoot's drummer and drummer on some of Stan Rogers's early recordings — worked for RCA Records in the early 1970s. He says that things weren't all bad. "In those days, it was easier for a Canadian artist to get a recording contract. One single was easy and cheap to produce, and the risks were lower. We'd slap a song on a record, put a name on it, and see what would happen."

The catch was that in order to get a contract, artists often had to hand their publishing rights over to the record company. In other words, the artists gave away ownership of their songs. This is an important concession because every time a song gets played on the radio or performed in concert, its owner gets a residual.

"From a publishing standpoint, it made more sense to sign a singer-songwriter," Keane says. "It's because of the MAPLe system. If you sang and wrote the song, that qualified you right away. Radio stations had to play your record, because it met their Cancon requirements, so even if you didn't sell any of those records, just having them played on the radio provided income."

Enter Stan Rogers. By 1970, Stan had dropped out of university for a second time — rumour has it he was kicked out for hitting a professor — and was trying his luck at teachers' college in Hamilton. As a profession, teaching was a reasonable compromise; it was acceptable to Stan's family and it satisfied Stan's own pedantic tendencies. And then there was the added benefit of summers off.

Faced with the prospect of a serious career, Stan decided to take one more kick at the musical can. He and Nigel Russell sent a demo tape to RCA's Toronto office. Within weeks, Stan got a phone call from the the head man at RCA; he had himself a deal.

Stan recorded his first single for RCA in the fall of 1970. It was a rush job; RCA wanted to have the record out in time for the Christmas market. The B side was the traditional "Coventry Carol," and the lead single was an original called "Here's To You, Santa Claus." The premise was that Santa, with his share-the-wealth attitude, must be a communist. The story is told from the point-of-view of an "all-American kid" who decides to take the Santa problem into his own hands.

> Hail to you Santa Claus flying up so high
> And if you come 'round here tonight
> I'll blast you from the sky
> If you get by my toy radar dome
> I'll grant you I can tell.
> The land mine in the fireplace will
> Blow you straight to hell.

While Stan was happy to have a recording contract, from the start he was uncomfortable with what the record company had in mind for him. Stan saw himself as a serious folk musician, but RCA saw him as novelty — Canada's answer to Burl Ives. This was a problem that plagued Stan his entire career; his talent was unique and defied established market labels.

While Stan wasn't happy with RCA's direction, he buckled down and went to work. The single was recorded at RCA's famous Mutual Street Studio in Toronto during a marathon forty-eight hour session. The recording went smoothly, Stan taking to the studio like a seasoned pro. As a matter of fact, things went better than Stan could have imagined. As he was improvising some lyrics for the lead single, the door opened and a familiar-looking man walked in. It took a moment to sink in, but all at once Stan realized who it was: his idol Gordon Lightfoot.

Of all the recording artists who influenced Stan Rogers's musical development, none had a more profound effect than Lightfoot.

Born in Orillia, Ontario, on November 17, 1938, Lightfoot was, like Rogers, a musical prodigy. When he was twenty, Lightfoot went to music college in Los Angeles, acquiring the theoretical background that most of his songwriting contemporaries lacked. By the early 1960s, Lightfoot was living in Toronto and proving his versatility. He sang in the coffee houses, arranged the music for commercials, and even contributed his square dance talents to the CBC TV show "Country Hoedown."

He also turned his attention to songwriting. It was the height of the folk boom, and Lightfoot's songs were quickly picked up by Canadian folk artists. Ian and Sylvia were impressed with Lightfoot's work and introduced the young singer-songwriter to their manager Albert Grossman.

The year 1965 was a watershed for Lightfoot. Peter, Paul and Mary's recording of his song "For Lovin' Me" was a top thirty hit in the U.S., while Marty Robbins' version of "Ribbon Of Darkness" reached number one on the country charts. Lightfoot signed a record contract with the American label and released his self-titled debut album.

For a young Canadian folk singer like Stan Rogers, it was a tremendous lift to see one of his countrymen make the big time. Stan listened to all of Lightfoot's albums over and over, and was particularly impressed with the song "Canadian Railroad Trilogy," from the 1967 album *The Way I Feel*. A historical ballad, it uses many elements that would later be found in Stan's best work including a complicated musical structure and a focus on that Canadian obsession, the link between transportation and communication.

Lightfoot nodded to Stan and took a seat in the control

room. He'd been in the studio next door, doing the final mix on his album *Sit Down Young Stranger*. He was a friend of Bill Misener, Stan's producer, and had come to check out the new talent.

As Nigel Russell recalls, Lightfoot cracked up listening to the words of "Here's To You, Santa Claus," and made a couple of joking suggestions of his own. After Stan's session was finished, Lightfoot invited the two young musicians to join him in his studio. It was just the four of them: Stan, Nigel, Lightfoot and the engineer. For Stan, who was then only twenty-two years old, the day was a dream come true.

But the next day, Stan came stumbling back to reality. He showed up at his class Friday morning, still tired from two days in the studio. The instructor confronted him immediately. "I was making a record for RCA." Stan hoped the professor would be duly impressed and let the matter drop.

"Will this be a regular occurrence?"

Stan shrugged his shoulders, "I hope so."

The teacher took off his glasses and offered Stan a long, penetrating look. Stan would have to make a decision, he said: "Music or teaching; you can't do both."

Stan smiled, slightly embarrassed by his own discomfort, but more than a little relieved. If only every decision in life could be this easy.

Home Brew

Hello London,
I just had to let you hear,
That my new friends are the best I've ever known
And I just might make this London town my home.
                              "Hello London," unreleased

The audience sat in rapt attention. Smale's Pace Folk Club was the most popular stop on London's burgeoning folk circuit. It was a classic coffee house of the early seventies, a hippy's idea of a home away from home. Cheap food, soup and sandwiches mostly, perhaps the occasional low level drug transaction, and cup after cup of strong coffee. That night the crowd was in for a special treat.

Stan took his seat, tuned his guitar for a few moments. It was February 1972 and he'd moved to London following a couple of career setbacks. His contract with RCA was terminated after his second single flopped and his partnership with Nigel Russell ended when Russell went solo.

Once his guitar was in tune, Stan spoke to the audience. "After you've lived in Hamilton for a number of years, you can appreciate what London is all about. It's nice to have air that you can breathe, and people who smile at you. It's also nice being able to share music with some good people. I just wrote a tune about it..."

Hello London,
Had to get back to see you again.
Already I find, I leave behind
The dusty steel mill city that was mine.

Stan sat back in his chair, his eyes closed, the room completely silent, except for the two guitars and the sound of his
voice. Although they were both part of Cedar Lake, Stan had
never shared a stage with Doug McArthur before. In fact, they
hadn't even rehearsed their set.

But that's what Cedar Lake was all about. A loose
arrangement of musicians — at any given moment, it ranged
from eight to twenty members — who got together to showcase their collective talents. They were young men, friends,
compatriots and for them the moment was everything.

Hello London,
I just had to let you hear,
That my new friends are the best I've ever
    known
And I just might make this London town
    my home.

For one brief moment, London was the centre of
Canada's folk universe. Some of the finest young singer-song-
writers gathered in this white collar city, where education
and finance are the main industries. Many of the names are
still familiar to folk fans: Gord Lowe, David Essig, Paul Mills,
David Bradstreet, Willie P. Bennett, Luke Gibson, Doug
McArthur, Frank Wheeler, Jim Ogilvie, Brent Titcomb. Even
Garnet Rogers caught the tail end of the London folk comet.
Other performers who made regular stops in London
included such luminaries as Bruce Cockburn, Murray
McLauchlan, and Valdy.

Cedar Lake was the drawing card, and it was the kind of

musical collective that only could have emerged in the early seventies. The name tells it all: it was deliberately generic, evoking an image of a pastoral Anytown, Canada. The good-will spilled over to the audience, who were as "into" the music as the performers. As Paul Mills recalls, it was the perfect place for a developing musician.

"We had the luxury of an audience that would come to the coffee house and sit through almost anything, and at least appear like they were enjoying themselves. Those were very self-indulgent days. Head down, eyes closed, everybody really got into the music. For all of us, the stage at Smale's Pace was like a school. We made our mistakes on that very forgiving stage and learned our craft."

As a performer and an artist, Cockburn, born in Ottawa in 1945, is in many ways the antithesis of Stan Rogers. Where Stan was gregarious and outspoken, Cockburn is aloof, a serious and studied musician. His interest in music was sparked in Grade 10 when he got his first guitar. While he obviously listened to pop and folk music of the time, Cockburn was also strongly influenced by jazz artists like Herb Ellis and Oscar Peterson. In the mid-sixties, Cockburn moved to Boston, where he began formal studies.

Cockburn has always had a strong commercial sense, and from the beginning of his career has written songs that are both artistic *and* popular. He was a national sensation in the seventies and made inroads in the United States in the eighties, charting several albums and singles. Cockburn is now recognized by music fans around the world. Though he lacks the lyrical and vocal prowess of some of his contemporaries, Cockburn is nevertheless one of the most important figures in contemporary Canadian music. Serious, political, wondrously melodic, he has become as much a voice for the urban experience as Stan was for the rural.

With his working class background and country music sensibility, Murray McLauchlan is much closer to Stan than Cockburn. McLauchlan was born in 1948 in Scotland, and moved to Canada at the age of five. By 17, he was playing coffee houses, and in the late sixties was signed to Canada's independent True North label, the same record company that signed Bruce Cockburn.

Unlike Rogers, though, McLaughlan's music was much more accessible to radio. In 1973 — a stellar year for domestic singles — McLauchlan's "The Farmers Song" became the hit that launched his career as a popular artist. But he was soon pegged as a country singer, and in an effort to reach a broader audience he released *Boulevard* in 1976. The album had a rockier edge than his earlier work, featured a full scale back-up band, and managed to crack the top 100.

McLaughlan has recorded almost twenty albums in twenty years. More recently he has moved into broadcasting. His popular CBC Radio show, "Swinging On A Star," brings the best of an eclectic range of acoustic music to Canadian audiences every week. Perhaps this is McLauchlan's way of keeping alive the spirit of the coffee houses where he began — the spirit of musical challenge and celebration.

♪   ♪   ♪

In London, Stan settled down after five years of restless wandering. He had found a circle of friends who accepted him, not just because of his talent, but because they *liked* him. Stan lived with a couple of transplanted Nova Scotians, brothers Mike and Tim Curry. Apparently, he went to the brothers' place for brunch one Sunday. During the course of the day, five gallons of home brew disappeared and the brothers had found themselves a new roommate.

STAN ROGERS MARITIME HOME BREW

This straightforward grog was Stan's favourite. The measurements aren't very precise — it's taken from Stan's handwritten recipe — but Ariel assures me that, with a little experimentation, you'll be able to make a simple and reliable home brew.

(1) Start yeast (lukewarm sugared water).
(2) Fill dutch oven 3/4 full with water.
       Place on high heat.
(3) Add: 1 bag dextrose
       1 can malt
       1 teaspoon salt
       1 teaspoon citric acid
       1 teaspoon finings
(4) Stir until finings dissolve. Then pour
       in vat.
(5) Add 4 1/2 dutch ovens of cool water.
(6) Stir in yeast.
(7) Cover.
(8) Let beer sit for at least 2 weeks. Then
       skim off foam and bottle.
(9) Add 1 teaspoon sugaring solution
       (see below) per bottle.

Sugaring solution:
       3/4 cup boiling water
       7 tablespoons sugar. Stir until dis-
       solved.

The house they shared defined Stan's London experience. It was a freelance flophouse-cum-performance-centre. The music would go on well into the night. And in the morning you'd have to step lightly over all the sleeping bodies to get your bowl of cereal. Rumour has it that Willie P. Bennett lived in a closet in this house for a time, when he had nowhere else to go. It was the kind of place where there was always a pot of stew on the stove, where the homemade beer flowed freely (average consumption: ten gallons a week) and rent was an afterthought.

Stan's closest friend in London was Paul Mills — no relation to Alan. The two first met in a university coffee house. Paul was studying to be an engineer at the time, but he was also a damn fine picker. He and Stan got to talking, hit it off, and wound up jamming until six in the morning.

It was Paul's suggestion that Stan move to London. By that time, Paul had nearly finished his MA and came to the distressing realization that he had no interest in being an engineer. Early one morning, as the last of the stragglers was clearing out of Stan's house, the two friends were finishing off a bottle of Scotch.

Out of the blue, Paul spoke up. "Well, I know what I want to do with my life." Stan put down his glass and looked at Paul, waiting for the punchline. There wasn't any. Paul really had made up his mind. "I want to be a record producer," he declared.

Stan looked pleased and, without missing a beat, suggested that Paul produce the albums Stan one day hoped to record. They shook on it and finished the bottle of Scotch. It was an unassuming start to a working partnership that would last for the rest of Stan's life.

Ariel

After twenty-three years you think I could
    find
A way to let you know somehow
That I want to see your smiling face forty-
    five years from now.
                    "Forty-Five Years," from *Fogarty's Cove*

I n the comfort of his new-found home, Stan was getting
back in touch with his Maritime roots. Before London, Stan
rarely mentioned the East Coast, and, as a teenager, he seldom visited there. But now, the Maritimes appealed to the
young man's sense of history and his romantic nature. Stan included a couple of old-time jigs in his act and would refer to
Nova Scotia as "the place where I come from." In Mike Curry's
words, "Stan considered himself to be a Nova Scotian and bit-
terly resented the fact that he wasn't born there."

Stan spent as much free time in Nova Scotia as he could
and particularly enjoyed his Uncle Prescott Rogers's little
cottage at Half Way Cove, just a short drive out of Hazel
Hill, Nova Scotia. It is here that in late September of 1973
Stan took Diane "Ariel" McEwen, whom he'd started dating
earlier that summer. Ariel was a nurse who was active in
the arts scene around Hamilton. They had met when Ariel
hired Stan to play at "It's Your Bag Day," a local arts festival,
and Stan was immediately taken by her red hair and fiery
personality.

Actually, it wasn't the first time they met. She had seen him years before playing in a coffee house and since then they'd seen each other occasionally in church in Hamilton. Their first formal introduction was in the summer of 1970, when Stan was assistant cook at a church camp and Ariel, who'd been camp nurse the summer before, was visiting. One of the girls took Ariel down to the cookhouse to meet Stan, who was asleep. Ariel was introduced to his feet, hanging limply over the end of the bed. So, it wasn't exactly love at first sight, but when they finally did get together, it was love nevertheless.

The weekend at Uncle Prescott's was one of laughter and discovery for the young lovers. And even after Ariel left, Stan felt her presence in that tiny house by the sea. A song was writing itself in his head and slowly made its way onto paper.

> Where the earth shows its bones of wind-
> broken stone
> And the sea and sky are one
> I'm caught out of time, my blood sings
> with wine
> And I'm running naked in the sun.

The result was "Forty-Five Years," a masterful love song. Later Stan would say that this was the only love song he ever wrote, but this was not strictly true. He wrote dozens of them in his early years, having learned the lesson of many young troubadours — that the quickest way into a girl's heart, and bedroom, was to write her a song. Stan's best songs were always "love songs" of a sort; they didn't speak of mythical or romantic love, the mainstay of pop music. Instead they dealt with the complicated, often ambiguous, and very real relationships we experience in our daily lives.

As "Forty-Five Years" was forming in Stan's mind, he sat down and wrote Ariel a letter which offers a revealing glimpse into Stan's creative process. The images and ideas that would soon make up the song permeate the letter like spirits, waiting to be given form. Stan writes:

> . . . Now that you've been here, and I've seen how you took to the place, I'm sure there will be a next time — many next times. I love you more than I ever thought possible, or mere words could ever say. But I've a song running up today, and this one I'm sure I'll keep.
>
> I just want to hold you closer than I've ever held anyone before.
>
> Mom says hi, and I hope you get back alright, and I overheard Dad telling my uncle Jim yesterday that "Stan's new girl-friend is really a pleasant type to have around." Whatever that means. I guess that's high praise coming from him.
>
> So far today I've had four cigarettes, and I'm about to light my fifth, which will be my last until after supper. Not bad, I guess. Funny as I sit here writing, the words to the song are coming faster and faster. Pretty soon I'll have to stop for a while and go find that dried up old guitar.
>
> Oh, love, I'll never forget the sight of you running naked and laughing in the sun with the water streaming down your breasts. I've never seen anything so beautiful in my life, and I've never seen anyone so happy. I'm sure you deserve that kind of happiness, but I'm not sure I deserve it.
>
> I'm still constantly amazed every time I think of the two of us together. I've never thought of myself as good looking, or as being particularly desirable to

women, and to find myself loving and being loved by one of the finest women a man could hope to meet is almost miraculous. I can see myself looking into those green eyes of yours fifty years from now, and loving it . . .

Enclosed with the letter, Ariel found two sheets of notepaper on which Stan had written the lyrics to his newest song, "Forty-Five Years."

> And I just want to hold you closer than
> I've ever held anyone before
> You say you've been twice a wife and
> you're through with life
> Ah, but Honey, what the hell's it for?
> After twenty-three years you'd think I
> could find
> A way to let you know somehow
> That I want to see your smiling face forty-
> five years from now.

The Guysborough Line

Now there's no train to Guysborough
Or so the man said
So it might be a good place to be.
     "Guysborough Train," CBC Transcription Series EP

By the end of 1973, all the pieces were in place. Stan had friends, musical cohorts and a family of sorts having moved in with Ariel and her three children — David, the oldest at four, Beth and Kate. The predator was being domesticated and didn't seem to mind it one bit.

"He was drawn to the kids like a moth to a flame," Ariel says. "He would lay on the couch for hours with Kate, just reading to her or talking or playing. It answered something inside him. People would ask him how he could take on this woman and her three kids. But he found something in it that was vital; it was absolutely like breathing to him."

As Stan was settling in with home life, his recording career was also starting to take shape. His friend Paul Mills had been hired as producer with CBC Radio and managed to wangle some studio time for Stan. In those days — before the Conservative Government decimated the CBC — it wasn't unusual for the "Corp" to record promising artists like Stan. The CBC had a mandate as a public broadcaster to promote and develop Canadian talent. In Stan's case, an EP record was produced for the in-house Transcription Series label.

Stan's three-song EP for CBC turned out to be his most successful recording venture to date. The songs were "pastoral pop" rather than pure folk music, as the opening lines of the lead song "Three Pennies" indicates.

> When day comes
> On this mountain
> To your well I will go
> Drink of you deep
> Watch you in sleep
> And down meadows green will softly
>   go . . .

Stan was trying to be a seventies mellow singer-songwriter, in the mold of James Taylor. But Stan did not have a confessional personality. The best he could achieve was a vague spiritual awareness that he tried to explain in the second song "Past Fifty."

> I'm going through life like a pilgrim
> Lost in the storm
> With winds that blow to make me
>   cold, but the holy body keeps
>   me warm.

In terms of melody, these two songs aren't bad for a young songwriter, but the lyrics don't stack up to Stan's later work. However, the third song was a stand out. "Guysborough Train" became a favourite of CBC programmers and was soon a hot commodity on the folk music black market. Everybody and their uncle-in-law begged, borrowed or bootlegged a copy.

The idea for the song was based in fact. In the 1960s, the Nova Scotia government promised to build a rail line to Guysborough, a town at the foot of Chedabucto Bay, and, like many government promises, this one was broken.

Now there's no train to Guysborough
Or so the man said
So it might be a good place to be.
I sit in this station
And I count up my change
And I wait for the Guysborough
        train.

The song has a political basis, but Stan was more interested in the futile imagery of a train going nowhere than he
was in the politics. The lyrics to "Guysborough Train" are
particularly interesting, because of Stan's use of the personal, narrative voice, the "I witness." While other folk
singers of the era used this kind of voice to explore their own
inner feelings — songwriting as therapy — Stan used it to
describe a historic event. In a sense, he was combining the
seventies singer-songwriter style with a traditional form, the
historical ballad.

And I ride for all time
On the Guysborough line
And I grow by the North County
        rain
And the North Shore's begun
The man I've become
In rags, on the Guysborough train.

"Guysborough Train" doesn't have the scope or impact
of a true historical ballad. But it was the starting point from
which Stan developed his literate and literary style of songwriting: song as story. The narrative voice is always slightly
detached, like Stan himself often felt, an observer on the edge
of circumstance.

The Smell of Success

Now, it's so tantalizing, this little smell of success . . .
The monkey demon keeps me screaming, and he won't let me
    rest
Oh, someone, won't you listen, and help drive the demons
    away?

"Try Like The Devil," from *Turnaround*

For the next two years, Stan worked hard to establish himself on the Canadian music scene. He had been touring extensively with a trio that included an old Cedar Lake crony on bass, Jim Ogilvie, and younger brother Garnet on fiddle, flute and electric guitar. They played every bar and folk club that would have them, and success seemed within their reach.

He took a second stab at a recording career, signing briefly with New York's prestigious folk music label Vanguard Records. Stan didn't stay with Vanguard for long, as Paul Mills recalls.

"The recording sessions did not go well. I think the problem was that we were all trying too hard. It ended up sounding forced. Vanguard insisted on hearing the rough mixes of the basic tracks and it was on the basis of these unfinished tracks that Vanguard decided to let Stan go."

In the early seventies, the dream of these developing musicians was to play the Mariposa Folk Festival. In folk music history, Mariposa ranks second only to the Newport Folk Festival in Rhode Island in terms of impact and longevity. It began like all great Canadian cultural events, as a tourism initiative. Ruth Jones conceived of the festival as a way to attract visitors to Orillia, Ontario, a town several hours north of Toronto. Both Gordon Lightfoot and humourist Stephen Leacock came from Orillia. The festival was named after Leacock's fictitious name for the city.

The first Mariposa Festival took place in 1961 and included such performers as Ian and Sylvia, who helped organize it, and Ed McCurdy, a singer of traditional Canadian songs. It was a mild success. Two thousand folk fans turned out, and, although the organizers lost money, the festival continued to grow. By 1964, the festival was so big that Orillia's city council banned it. It changed locations for several years before finding a new home in 1968 on the Toronto Islands.

Estelle Klein was Mariposa's artistic director from the mid-sixties through to the end of the seventies. The festival was originally all-Canadian, out of financial necessity more than any philosophical disposition. Later Klein felt a broad base was important and, though she was criticized by some, transformed the festival into an international showcase.

The Mariposa Festival was a product of the folk boom, and throughout its history this was reflected in a tendency toward "pure" traditional music and a focus on performances as opposed to performers. Acts were generally given half-hour timeslots, and multi-performer workshops were the order of the day. To discourage any sort of star system from developing, there were no evening shows. The 1972 calendar of events makes this point abundantly clear:

All Programs
end at 8:30
.... pm .....
Festival Site
must be cleared
at this time

As the seventies drew to a close, Mariposa began to lose impact. Soon Mitch Podolak's Winnipeg festival surpassed it in importance, leading the way for a host of regional festivals in Vancouver, Sudbury, Owen Sound, London and more. By the early eighties, Mariposa had just about fizzled out. In 1984 the floundering festival moved to Barrie, Ontario, under the sponsorship of Molson's Brewery, where it was plagued by bad weather, spotty attendance, and an unfamiliar location. It eventually returned to Toronto, this time to Ontario Place, but the bad weather and sparse crowds followed.

By the summer of 1975, the hard work began to pay off, as Stan moved on to the folk festival circuit. It was a good opportunity, since festivals were the proving ground for folk artists. One great show at Mariposa or Winnipeg could establish an artist's international reputation.

Stan played four major festivals that year: Blue Skies in Clarendon Station near Kingston, Ontario; Home County in London; Mariposa; and Winnipeg. Mariposa was still the most important festival in the country. But Stan believed that the Mariposa organizers put undue emphasis on traditional folk music and he agreed only reluctantly to participate.

During the mid-seventies, a new kind of folk music was having an impact on radio, with James Taylor and Carole King taking the lead. The prerequisites for this "singer-song-writer" movement included simple arrangements — acoustic guitars preferred — and a self-accompanied artist whose original songs featured rich, introspective lyrics. These days, the labels "singer-songwriter" and "folk singer" have become almost interchangeable.

In Canada, record companies and radio programmers didn't know what to make of these contemporary folk singers. This uncertainty resulted in a number of syrupy pop singers getting record deals, but also opened radio up to a number of genuine folk performers such as Bruce Cockburn and Murray McLauchlan — who at that time were both recording for True North, one of the very few successful independent record companies ever to come out of Canada.

Valdy, a contemporary of Cockburn and McLaughlan, is

another interesting example of a successful singer-songwriter. He was one of the first national folk artists to break top forty radio format, achieving this success despite — or perhaps because of — his decision to live outside of Southern Ontario's major entertainment markets.

Born Valdemar ,Horsdal, and originally from Ottawa, Valdy came to epitomize the hippy ideal: sort of a one-man version of Cedar Lake. A resident of Saltspring, an island halfway between Vancouver and Victoria, he sang songs with titles like "Country Man," "Simple Life," and "Hometown Band." Valdy's easy manner and smooth singing style allowed him to straddle the gulf between folk and popular music.

Although he had been involved in the folk music scene since the mid-sixties, it wasn't until 1971 that he made an impact on radio with the single "Rock And Roll Song." What followed was a succession of top forty singles and top-selling albums.

Despite his achievements, today Valdy considers the "folk" stereotype a detriment.

"I have found this designation to be one hundred-and-ten percent limiting. My manager said, 'DO NOT USE THE WORD FOLK.' But I never listened. And here we are twenty years later and my manager is still saying, 'We are not using the word folk.' "

What concerned Valdy's manager was the public's ambivalence towards folk music. It had come in and out of fashion numerous times before; the public's taste would undoubtedly change again.

Valdy and folk singers like him impressed Stan, who realized that if he ever wanted to make it, he had to crack the radio markets. Once again, the CBC entered the picture. The "Guysborough Train" EP had been so popular that Paul Mills got the go-ahead to make another record with Stan. What at first seemed a golden opportunity for Stan developed into one of the most traumatic episodes in both their recording careers.

The studio was booked for ten o'clock on a snowy morning not long after New Year's Day, 1976. By 10:30, Stan hadn't arrived. At eleven o'clock, still nothing. It was snowing

heavily that day and the radio reported numerous road-clo-
sures and a rash of serious accidents. As it neared 11:30, Paul
contemplated calling off the session.

"I had a room full of musicians who were getting paid and
I was responsible for the budget. When Stan and the boys
finally arrived, they were all flustered. They unpacked their
instruments and started to play. It was just awful. Stan was so
agitated that he couldn't play his guitar. Jim Ogilvie's bass had
something wrong with it; there was a buzz in one of the strings.
Nothing was going right."

At that point, with time and money rapidly disappear-
ing, a stressed-out Paul Mills was forced to make an execu-
tive decision. He told Stan to put down his guitar. Paul
wanted Stan just to sing and asked Jim Ogilvie to take a
coffee break, effectively kicking the bass player out of the
studio. Paul then assigned studio musicians to play in place
of Jim and Stan.

After recording the track, Stan was livid. "How dare you
defile my music this way?" he demanded, barely containing
his rage. Paul explained that he was trying to do his job, but
that didn't cut much slack with Stan. He didn't speak to Paul
for three months and the friendship seemed all but over. Two
months after the incident, Paul got an angry letter from Stan.
At that time, Paul was producing the show "Touch the Earth"
for CBC.

"Stan wrote this four page letter, tearing me to shreds for
what I had done. The letter was about honesty and all the
things that mattered to him in terms of the music. The one
line I remember was: 'Touch the earth? You wouldn't know it
if it crawled into bed with you.' It was the biggest falling out
that Stan and I ever had."

The *other* effect was that Stan Rogers lost a bass player.
Jim Ogilvie had felt uncomfortable throughout the recording
session. They had been playing together for three years, but
suddenly Ogilvie felt like an outsider. This is his account of
what happened: "We had evolved the songs in our own fashion and, when we went in to record, that's how we were going
to play them. I tried to do it the way they wanted, but I didn't

really want to and I think that showed. Stan and I had a little squabble and it blew up. I left and that was it."

Stan had encountered the harsh reality of the business world. Despite the best of intentions and integrity, one is ruled by simple economics at the most inopportune moments. The result is often that people get hurt and friendships are shattered.

Revival

God damn them all!
I was told we'd cruise the seas for American gold
We'd fire no guns! Shed no tears!
But I'm a broken man on a Halifax pier
The last of Barrett's Privateers.

"Barrett's Privateers," from *Fogarty's Cove*

Fans know Stan Rogers as a songwriter and singer, but few appreciate the impact he's had on folk music in general. Other artists, such as Leonard Cohen, used traditional motifs in their music, but Stan went much further. He was a modern-day trailblazer, who almost single-handedly established a Canadian folk idiom, and helped spark interest in British and Celtic music that swept across North America. Because of Stan, we've all come to recognize that there are other "American" forms of music besides country and the blues. There are jigs, reels, shanties, broadside ballads, hornpipes — all of which deserve a place, not just in music history, but in contemporary songwriting as well.

Although Stan was a child of the American folk boom of the early 1960s, his model was the so-called "Brit Trad revival" in Britain during the early 1970s.

The folk boom of the early sixties was by-and-large an American phenomenon that had a limited effect on British popular music. There was "skiffle" in the late fifties, which combined elements of American traditional music — simple instruments like acoustic guitars and washboards and songs by the likes of Leadbelly and Woody Guthrie — with British dance band sensibilities. The skiffle craze swept through England, and many of Britian's pop music heavyweights, such as Lennon and McCartney, cut their teeth in skiffle bands. British traditionalists resented the American origins of skiffle and sought to revive their own musical heritage.

This "Brit Trad revival" was spearheaded by Bert Lloyd, a musicologist and singer, and Ewan MacColl, a singer and songwriter of distinction, whose elegant ballad "The First Time Ever I Saw Your Face" was a hit for Roberta Flack in 1971. The idea was to incorporate the traditional music of the British Isles in contemporary rock and folk forms. Brit Trad gained momentum in the early seventies, with the rise of bands such as Fairport Convention, Incredible String Band and Steeleye Span. Its influence could be heard in the generations of artists that followed, such as the Clash, U2, the Pogues and Billy Bragg.

♪   ♪   ♪

In Canada, the unofficial homebase for the British revival music was a coffee house in Toronto called Fiddler's Green. The club was formed in 1970 by a group of transplanted Brits that included Tam Kearney and Jim Strickland. It quickly became one of the most popular folk music venues in the city. Grit Laskin is a guitar maker and a member of the Friends of Fiddler's Green, the club's house band.

Laskin remembers the club in all its glory: "Technically the building was condemned, but we used it anyway. The upper floors shouldn't have been stepped on, but we had a secret way to get in and set up our equipment. When it was at its peak, it was running two nights a week, and each night was so jammed that there were line-ups in the parking lot. It was crazy; we would pack in over 120 people, way beyond any type of fire code limit."

Stan was a frequent visitor to Fiddler's Green. Even if he

wasn't featured on the bill, he would show up and just join in. He loved the atmosphere of the club: the performances were free-flowing and the club's format was as loose as its floorboards. It was a sharp contrast to Stan's polished and well-practised stage show.

One of the Fiddler's Green regulars was a mysterious guitarist and singer who went by the name Leon Redbone. Redbone is interesting both as a folk artist and as an example of the difficulties the general public has in understanding folk idioms. Unlike the other Fiddler's Green regulars, Redbone wasn't into the Brit Trad revival. Many would say that he wasn't even a folk artist because he was an interpreter of pop songs from the thirties and forties and even earlier. His repertoire included "Ain't Misbehavin'," "When You Wish Upon A Star" and "Your Cheating Heart," and begged the question: Is it folk?

Leon Redbone became a pop music sensation in 1976, thanks in part to Bob Dylan's outspoken support and to a timely appearance on TV's "Saturday Night Live." Part of Redbone's appeal was his air of mystery: he looked like a Lebanese Groucho Marx, had a taciturn disposition, rarely gave interviews and always wore dark glasses. His enigmatic ways weren't just for show; he always surrounded himself in secrecy. Redbone's playful profile from the 1972 Mariposa Festival program is a good example:

> I was born in Shreveport, LA in 1910, and my real name is James Hokum. I wear dark glasses to remind me of the time I spent leading Blind Blake throughout the south, and I now live in Canada as a result of the incident in Philadelphia.

In response to a request for a photograph for the program, Redbone sent a crumpled snapshot of Bob Dylan.

In 1976, Redbone made *On The Track* for Warner

Brothers. Over the next ten years, he released half a dozen albums. He started out as the darling of music critics and record buyers, but with each album their disenchantment grew. Fewer and fewer albums sold, although most made the top forty chart. Meanwhile, critics concluded that he was nothing more than a novelty act whose novelty had worn off.

The problem for Redbone was that pop music demands change. Enduring pop artists, such as David Bowie, understand this dynamic and go to great pains to reinvent themselves. Folk artists who enter the mainstream always have a hard time staying there because folk, by its very nature, doesn't change. In the pop world, where craftsmanship and integrity are suspect, folk artists are soon relegated to "novelty act" status.

♪   ♪   ♪

Once Stan got the notion to become a one-man revival movement, he explored different traditional forms. His first success, however, came as much by accident as design. He was playing the Northern Lights Festival in Sudbury, Ontario, and between shows Stan would join the other performers, including the Friends of Fiddler's Green, for a beer and a song. Chorus songs were a favourite at this type of gathering: a leader sings the verse, then the group joins in for the chorus. Stan had one problem with chorus songs. Since he didn't know any, he was never able to sing lead, and there's only so long that Stan could stay in the background.

Ian Robb, a Friend of Fiddler's Green and one of Stan's favourite performers, was at the Northern Lights Festival. He recalls what happened that afternoon. "Stan liked the idea of chorus songs. For him, it was a big social scene; he really enjoyed hanging around with us and singing along. We were doing our usual singing around, and Stan was there. Finally Stan said with a smile, 'I've had enough of playing second fiddle to you guys!' and he went away."

No more than twenty minutes later, Stan returned to the group with a new song in his hands. It was called "Barrett's Privateers," and from the moment Stan sang the first line, it was obvious that he had just created a modern classic.

> Oh, the year was 1778,
> (How I wish I was in Sherbrooke now!)
> A letter of marque came from the king
> To the scummiest vessel I've ever seen.

Fogarty's Cove

She will walk the sandy shore so plain
Watch the combers roll in
Til I come to Wild Rose Chance again
Down in Fogarty's Cove.
                    "Fogarty's Cove," from *Fogarty's Cove*

You know, Stan..." June Jarvis placed a bowl full of homemade Blueberry Grunt in front of her ever-hungry nephew. "I was just thinking..."

Stan scooped a spoonful of blueberry and biscuit into his mouth. "Well, don't hurt yourself."

Aunt June continued. "You spend so much time down around Canso, it's like a second home."

Stan grunted. Apparently the dessert was having its desired effect.

"I mean, you're always looking for something to write about. Why don't you write some songs about right here?"

BLUEBERRY GRUNT

This dessert, one of Stan's favourites, comes courtesy of his aunt June Jarvis. She explains the significance of the name: "The idea is that you eat so much of it that all you can do is push your bowl away and grunt."

(1) Mix 3 parts blueberries (fresh preferred) to 1 part white sugar.
(2) Cook on low until sugar is dissolved and berries are boiling.
(3) Drop spoon-sized blobs of sweet biscuit dough into the mixture, just like adding dumplings to a stew. Add two blobs per serving.
(4) Cover. Cook on low heat for 12 minutes.
(5) Serve, when just cool enough to eat, with cream or vanilla ice cream.
(6) Eat until full. Then grunt.

♪   ♪   ♪

In 1974, at his Aunt June's suggestion, Stan tried his hand at writing a song about the Eastern Shore. It was a simple idea, but it proved to be an important step in Stan's career, the beginning of a process that culminated in his 1976 debut album *Fogarty's Cove.*

Stan had written songs about Nova Scotia before — "Guysborough Train," "Pocketful Of Gold," "Going Home" were about the Maritimes. But "Fogarty's Cove" was different. It wasn't just *about* the Maritimes; the song itself had the feel of traditional Maritime music.

Stan made a demo of "Fogarty's Cove" that summer, recording it in the basement studio of an aspiring young producer, Danny Lanois. In the 1980s, Lanois emerged as one of the world's top producers and worked with artists like U2, Bob Dylan, the Neville Brothers and Robbie Robertson.

At that time, Paul Mills had just started producing CBC Radio's "Touch the Earth," hosted by Sylvia Tyson. The show quickly became a popular and influential program that helped advance Stan's career. Directly, he got national exposure from his numerous appearances. Indirectly, "Touch the Earth" brought Stan together with Mitch Podolak, the driving force behind his first album.

Podolak, a freelance journalist from Winnipeg, approached Mills with an idea. He told Paul that he wanted to start a folk festival in Winnipeg, and asked the producer to chip in some of his budget to get the ball rolling. To Mitch's surprise, Paul said yes. Thus the CBC, through Paul Mills, was the first to offer financial support to the Winnipeg Folk Festival.

From the start, Winnipeg was a different kind of festival than Mariposa. The focus was more on the performers than on the music itself, which suited Stan fine. While Mariposa was a product of the sixties' folk boom, which had strong ties to the academic world, Winnipeg came out of the seventies, when tepid pop songs and disco's mechanical rhythms ruled radio. Festivals such as the Winnipeg Folk Festival provided a musical alternative, a place where music fans could rediscover the excitement of live music. Winnipeg proved to be the best of them all, and by the late seventies, it had surpassed Mariposa in prestige and influence.

In September of 1974, a month after the first Winnipeg Festival, Mitch Podolak was in Toronto. He decided he owed Paul Mills a phone call. The two met for dinner, and Paul brought along a tape of "Fogarty's Cove."

"I was sitting there listening to this tape and getting my mind blown," Podolak recalls. "So Paul called up Fiddler's Green where Stan was playing that night and said to Stan: 'Listen, when you're finished, get your ass over here right away. There's someone I want you to meet.' "

Mitch was so impressed that he invited Stan to play at the Winnipeg Folk Festival that following summer. Despite a serious case of the jitters, Stan was in top form. The audience was bowled over by the sheer energy of the man. Until Winnipeg, Stan had been a regional phenomenon with pockets of support in Southern Ontario and on the East Coast. Thanks to Winnipeg, the folk world sat up and took notice.

At some point during the festival, Mitch Podolak asked about Stan's recording career. How come an artist with Stan's obvious talent didn't have a record deal? The truth was that nobody was knocking on Stan's door. His music was so far out of the mainstream that even folk labels weren't interested in taking a chance on him. On the spur of the moment, Podolak had a great idea.

"I had five grand saved up," Podolak recalls. "I went to the bank and borrowed another $5000. With this money I started Barn Swallow Records and paid for Stan's first album. All of a sudden, I was a record company. And the best part was that I knew nothing about making records."

♪   ♪   ♪

Fogarty's Cove was recorded in September 1976, at the Springfield Sound studio in London, Ontario. The budget was tight, so the band had to work around the clock.

David Woodhead was Stan's bass player at the time. He recalls that the record was finished in, well, record time. "It took us two days to do Fogarty's Cove, which was unheard of back then. This really relates to Stan's professionalism. He liked to get the job done. But also, he did have a certain show-off quality. I think it was important to him to be able to do a record faster than anybody else."

Stan assembled his band and a crew of his old friends to help put Fogarty's Cove together. Paul Mills produced and performed under the alias Curly Boy Stubbs. John Allen Cameron appeared on one track, and Grit Laskin turned up on several tracks using the alias "The Masked Luthier Of Dupont Street." The reason for the false name was that Laskin didn't belong to the musician's union and, technically, couldn't play with other union musicians.

The songs on this album were influenced by Stan's numerous trips to Nova Scotia, and in particular by the work he did with his friend, the poet Bill Howell.

Stan wanted to use the album to start his own "Can Trad revival." Of the twelve songs on Fogarty's Cove, eleven relate to the East Coast. Howell was living in Nova Scotia at the time, and the two collaborated in an ongoing artistic experiment called "Anecdote," which aired periodically on the CBC Radio show "Music Maritimes." "Anecdote" had an interesting premise: the poet and songwriter carried on a "dialogue" through their artistic mediums. This "on demand" writing helped Stan hone his skill as a songwriter, while his close association with Howell gave Stan a greater understanding of the techniques of poetry. Several of the songs from "Anecdote" wound up on *Fogarty's Cove*.

Side One was a powerful introduction to an important new folk artist. It contained "Forty-Five Years," "Fogarty's Cove," and "Barrett's Privateers" — all stand-out tracks. The second side is a mini-suite that summarizes the range of Stan's Can Trad vision. The songs include the historical ballad "The Rawdon Hills," "Plenty Of Hornpipe," the first of many ship salvage songs "The Wreck Of The Athens Queen," "Make And Break Harbour" and a recitation, "Finch's Complaint." The side opens and closes with the haunting, Celtic-inspired song "Giant."

Considering that *Fogarty's Cove* was a young artist's first album, it is surprisingly dark and gloomy — folk gothic, as it were. In fact, the album is one long meditation on the relationship between vitality and decay.

Stan was particularly fascinated with working people: time and time again the people of his songs struggle to be productive, to make a buck, only to encounter forces of destruction. In "Maid On The Shore," sailors search for love and find death instead. In "Barrett's Privateers," one young man searches for wealth and winds up literally without a leg to stand on. In "The Rawdon Hills," all that's left from a Maritime gold rush are "the worn down shacks of labour past on a hill of broken stone." In "The Wreck Of The Athens Queen" the image of decay is reversed; a shipwrecked boat yields her treasures. In "Make And Break Harbour," the fish boats return with "a dry empty hold" and "too many are pulled up and rotten." And in "Finch's Complaint," the last piece on the album, Stan's mood is summed up; as the song's hero says, "We're working men with no work left to do."

In terms of Stan's career, the timing of *Fogarty's Cove* was perfect. The album — dedicated to Stan's grandfathers and to "the people of Canada's Atlantic Provinces" — was an ideal introduction for the record-buying market, because it presented a clear image of Stan Rogers that consumers could easily identify. The album almost worked too well. For the rest of his career, the general public recognized Stan not as a singer of songs about the Maritimes, but as a Maritime singer.

Turnaround

Bits and pieces you offered of your life
I didn't think they meant a lot or said much for you
And all the chances to follow didn't make a lot of sense
When stacked against the choices you made.

"Turnaround," from Turnaround

Fogarty's Cove was an immediate success. Stan sold 8,000 copies within nine months of its release, with a timely appearance on CBC's "Morningside" boosting sales. Critics also picked up on the album, and quickly recognized its importance. The Montreal *Gazette* called it "a superbly executed collection of songs about the Maritimes. . . . One of the finest folk music albums to yet come out of Canada." The L.A.-based *Folk Scene* singled out *Fogarty's Cove* as top contender for Best Folk Record of the Year and concluded it was "a great achievement in every respect." At a moment when folk music threatened to implode under the pressure of self-indulgence, Stan was a breath of fresh sea air.

Although *Fogarty's Cove* opened a lot of doors, Stan wasn't completely happy with the results. His knack for writing "authentic" songs and his attempt to establish a Canadian folk identity made him the darling of folk purists, a group which Stan had long avoided. He decided that what he needed was another album to showcase his versatility as a songwriter and prevent himself from being pigeon-holed.

Stan started recording his second album *Turnaround* in late September 1977, and finished just in time for his marriage to Ariel on the thirtieth of that month. The record was something of salvage job, an apt image since it is one that Stan returned to again and again in his songwriting. Stan searched through the songs he had written over the last ten years to find ones that would best represent his diverse songwriting repertoire. In the end, out of ten songs, only "The Jeannie C." was written specifically for the album.

The project began under the auspices of Mitch Podolak's Barn Swallow Records, but, after the recording began, Podolak pulled out. He simply had no more money. Without the cash, *Turnaround* seemed dead in the water.

Enter Stan's parents. Valerie had recently started up a mail-order business in her kitchen to help meet the demand for *Fogarty's Cove*. In reality, Valerie's decision wasn't completely voluntary. She started off mailing some albums for her son, just to help, and the next thing she knew, Stan presented her with a business licence and a vision of a corporate empire which would one day, he hoped, span recording, wholesale, retail managment and artist promotion.

The mail order side was going quite well. Buoyed by its success, Al and Valerie decided to take a bigger chance on their son. They invested part of their life savings to complete *Turnaround* and in the process started a new recording and publishing company called Fogarty's Cove Music. Having already made his money back on the first album, Mitch sold Barn Swallow Records to the new Rogers family label for $2,500, retaining half the publishing rights. Garnet, a talented graphic artist, sat down and designed the company logo: a boat on posts, out of the water, waiting for refitting and its ultimate return to the sea.

♪   ♪   ♪

Throughout his career, Stan struggled with the fact that, on the one hand, he wanted commercial success, while on the other, he didn't want to be seen as a "sell-out" to the folk

community. In other words, he wanted stardom without compromise. With *Turnaround*, Stan's struggle is clearly laid out:
one side features the traditional music his fans wanted to hear,
while the other offered the singer-songwriter material that
Stan hoped would get him radio play.

Side One contained work of the revivalist Stan: "Dark
Eyed Molly" by Scottish folksinger Archie Fisher and a version of the traditional "Oh No, Not I," which Stan described
as "folk punk" and earned the singer the nickname "Steeleye
Stan," a reference to the British revival band Steeleye Span.
"Second Effort" was a countrified tune culled from a CBC
Radio special "So Hard To Be So Strong." "Bluenose," originally written for a Government of Nova Scotia promotional
film, was actually one of Stan's least favourite from among his
Maritime tunes. But the final cut on Side One was a standout: "The Jeannie C." It's the story of an old fisherman who
loses his beloved boat to the sea, and along with "Barrett's
Privateers" and "Northwest Passage," it is one of Stan's most
powerful Can Trad songs.

Side Two of *Turnaround* is reserved for the singer-songwriter Stan. "So Blue" is an unabashed tribute to Canadian
Joni Mitchell, whose jazz-influenced songwriting style had a
tremendous impact on Stan. "The Front Runner," another
song rescued from *So Hard To Be So Strong*, and "Try Like The
Devil" both betray Stan's country roots. "The Song Of The
Candle," a hold-over from his pre-London days, showed that
Stan could be as introspective and as obscure as any other
singer-songwriter.

The title track, one of the first songs Stan ever wrote, finishes the album. Stan was very proud of the song but never
talked about the story behind it. Nigel Russell was there in
1969 when Stan wrote "Turnaround" and he interprets it as
an attempt by Stan to come to terms with his own limitations.
At the time it was written, the Hobbits had just broken up
and Stan was visiting Nigel in Peterborough. Nigel was going
out for a jog, and had tried unsuccessfully to talk an out-of-
shape Stan into joining him.

"After I'd gone a few blocks, I heard somebody call me;

I turned around, and there was Stan. He figured that he could catch me and keep up, even though he was totally out of shape. He figured that all he had to do was put his mind to it. But already he was fading, and when I looked at him, he had given up."

Never one to waste his energy, Stan went to work as soon as he got back to the house. By the time Nigel returned from his jog, Stan had finished composing "Turnaround."

> And if I had followed a little ways
> Because we're friends you would have
>   made me welcome out there.
> But we both know it's just as well,
>   'cause some can go
> But some are meant to stay behind,
>   and it's always that way.

Only by a fluke did Stan wind up including "Turnaround" on the album. They were nearing the end of the recording sessions and the crew was relaxing after dinner. Garnet started singing this half-forgotten song, and Mike Curry, who often showed up at the studio for moral support, loved it. At Curry's insistence, Stan put "Turnaround" on the album. And what began as an afterthought summed up the mood of the entire album, as well as pointing to the direction Stan's life was about to take.

Damn Yankees

In a few more years I won't remember what it was to play
The music of old friends who need to live so far away.
But can I once taste Northern waters, then forsake them for
    the South
To feel California's ashes in my mouth.
"California," from Northwest Passage

S tan had high hopes for *Turnaround*, but the public response was disappointing. The album sold reasonably well, thanks to Stan's touring and his mother's relentless mail-order work, but without the benefit of a show-stopper like "Barrett's Privateers" or "Forty-Five Years," *Turnaround* lacked bite. To this day, it remains one of Stan's least commercially successful albums.

Still, the album served its purpose. *Turnaround* established Stan as a reliable recording artist and as a songwriter of unlimited potential. And because they produced the album on the cheap, the family soon sold enough copies to break even.

The year 1978 started with a setback. David Woodhead, the bass player, announced that he was quitting the band. Stan should have seen it coming. Woodhead was a brilliant, creative player who liked musical challenges. He wasn't cut out to be Stan Rogers's sideman for life. It was too bad because, musically, the combination worked well. Stan provided a firm foundation which allowed Woodhead room to improvise. Meanwhile Garnet was developing into a superb accompanist, his relaxed manner and off-the-cuff remarks providing the perfect foil to his brother's more practised and measured performance.

In the trio, Stan had found a format which allowed him to present his best assets — his voice and songs — upfront and pushed his liabilities to the background. Once known for marble-mouthed song introductions and abrasive attempts at humour, Stan was now earning a reputation for his crisp, professional show.

♪   ♪   ♪

Soon after *Turnaround* was released, Stan started to make inroads into the United States. One of his earliest American fans was Emily Friedman, editor of the prestigious Chicago-based folk journal *Come For To Sing*. The two first met at the 1975 Winnipeg Folk Festival, although, as Friedman recalls, it was a rough introduction.

"I wound up being in an elevator with Stan. He was a little stand-offish at the time. What I didn't know was that Stan disliked America and Americans. So he barely acknowledged me."

Their next meeting went better. It was the following year, again in Winnipeg. But this time, when Stan saw her, he ran over to her and gave her one of his trademark bear hugs. Presumably he was pleased with the positive press he had gotten in her magazine.

In time, Friedman became a devoted and influential friend. Stan would often visit her when he was down in the States and became a regular columnist in her journal. Friedman sang his praises to anyone who would listen and even acted as his one-woman distribution company in the United States, selling albums from her living room.

Stan tried to get U.S. club dates numerous times. At first, no one wanted to book him. But as his reputation grew, Stan ran into a different obstacle: U.S. Immigration. Immigration seemed reluctant to give an unknown performer the proper papers, and Stan, unlike other performers, would not work in the U.S. without a visa. Stan was finally allowed to perform at a benefit concert for *Come For To Sing*. In the eyes of the U.S. government, as long as he wasn't making any money, he was welcome.

Among the first major American performers to recognize Stan's talent was Tom Paxton, a central figure in the sixties folk boom who remains a potent musical force to this day. Paxton was born in Chicago in 1937 and moved to Oklahoma as a youngster. In the early sixties, he hooked up with the Greenwich Village crowd which included Dylan, Phil Ochs, Pete Seeger, and Peter, Paul and Mary. And in 1965, he released the landmark folk album *Ramblin' Boy*.

Paxton's first introduction to Stan was at the 1978 Summerfolk Festival in Owen Sound, located about three hours northeast of Toronto on Georgian Bay. Paxton was walking across a field early on a Sunday morning.

"I heard this incredible voice coming over the loudspeaker, singing 'Amazing Grace.' This huge voice. And I thought, 'Who the hell is that?' Then I realized it must be Stan Rogers. I'd been hearing so much about him. Folk music is a very small world and we quickly get to hear about the people we haven't met yet. The word was out that he was a definite comer."

Paxton met Rogers a half hour later and they became friends. The American singer had a tremendous respect for Stan and considered Stan the Canadian equivalent of the American folk giant, Woody Guthrie. Paxton even wrote a song for Stan, now forgotten, although in Paxton's opinion there's no great loss since the song "turned out not to be very good."

Stan's immigration problems had a positive side. American folk fans were itching to get a look at him. His first major show was at the Philadelphia Folk Festival, the premier American festival since the decline of Newport in the late sixties.

As Garnet Rogers recalls, the band had a chip on its shoulder and set out to prove to the Americans just what they could do. "The festival organizers didn't want to give us an evening concert; they gave us a cheesy afternoon slot. We felt ill-used. We just had a bad attitude, brought about by three guys being in the same van year after year, grinding it out. We just decided that we were going to go out there and tear their faces off."

They parked their van in a secluded spot and just sat there with the windows shut, psyching themselves up for the show.

"We just huddled," Garnet continues. "Finally we opened the door of the van, fixed bayonets on our guitars, and went over the top."

These were the days when jeans and t-shirts were the standard folk uniform, but Stan's band dressed up for all their shows. In the end, they put on the kind of show that wouldn't be out of place at a rock concert.

"We'd leap around stage: three guys thrashing around, running from one end of the stage to the other. We finished the last chord of 'Witch of the Westmorland.' Everyone went nuts because we weren't just a bunch of folk singers up there farting around. Needless to say, they gave us the evening spot the next night."

Why was Stan an immediate hit with American audiences, while it took him years to catch on in Canada? For starters, his personality was probably better suited the American temperament. Like it or not, Canadians tend to be compliant and polite, two adjectives rarely used to describe Stan Rogers. On the contrary, he was brash and demanding, which is exactly how Americans expect talented people to behave.

And then there's the prodigal son theory: Canadians don't acknowledge their artists until they become successful somewhere else. At home, Stan was just another "wannabe," but in the States they recognized his merits without prejudice. In fact, being Canadian was a selling point in the United States. Stan seemed, well, exotic.

Because Canadians and Americans live so close together, sharing a common language and similar cultures, the differences between our two countries aren't always apparent. But

Nigel Russell, who grew up in Canada and now makes his home in Texas, says a performer can always tell what country he's in without looking at a map.

"Canadian audiences clap on the 'on' beat; American audiences clap on the 'off' beat. That's not a bad thing, except that Canadians feel bad for clapping on the 'on' beat. It doesn't sound right, because it's not what the Americans are doing."

This seems a small point, but performer after performer has commented on it. And it does suggest that at the very heart — for rhythm is the heartbeat of song — Canadians and Americans approach music differently. Given the number of Canadian songwriters who have found success in the States — Lightfoot, Mitchell, Cohen, Young, Robbie Robertson and Bachman-Cummings, among them — there must be some common quality or attribute that sets them apart.

Stan's friend and fellow folk singer Doug McArthur believes that the difference lies in Canadian songwriters' tendency to be less political and more literary than their American counterparts. "Canadians are perceived by American audiences as having a more balanced point of view. Canadians like to distance themselves from their subjects. In our country, we're physically so far apart from each other that we've become fascinated by distance; we are fascinated by the spaces inbetween."

Nigel Russell agrees. "Canadian songwriters have a view that comes from not having grown up in violent cities. It's the same kind of feel that country music has: heartfelt, optimistic and wholesome."

All these "Canadian" qualities are found in the music of Stan Rogers. At home, they often went unnoticed, but in the United States they added to his appeal.

Between the Breaks

We grow but grow apart —
We live but more alone —
The more to be, the more to see,
To cry aloud that we are free
To hide our ancient fears of being alone.
    "Delivery Delayed," from *Between the Breaks*

The world got a little bigger for Stan Rogers in 1979. He put out another album, his third in three years. He played major club dates and festivals throughout North America. And best of all, he became a father.

The new album was called *Between the Breaks*. It's dedicated to Emily Friedman, the friend who talked Stan into making a live record. She remembers: "I was hoping Stan would achieve that high-energy spontaneity on record that he had in his live performances, but which had been missing in his previous two albums. The production on his studio albums tended to drift further and further away from how he sounded live, as his career progressed. I thought a live album would be a great way to show off the songs."

The album was recorded in a restaurant-cum-folk club in Toronto, The Groaning Board. To fill out the sound, Stan expanded his usual complement of three musicians to five. Garnet was there, along with David Allen Eadie, the latest bass player. Grit Laskin joined in on an eclectic selection of instru-

ments that included the long-necked mandolin, Northum-
brian smallpipes, and the concertina. Curly Boy Stubbs, aka
Paul Mills, kicked in on guitar. Mills also retained his job as
producer, while his co-producer on "Touch the Earth," Bill
Garrett, lent a hand in the mobile recording truck.

The recordings took place over the span of four nights,
during what was one of the most hectic weeks in Stan's life.
He commented in the album's liner notes:

> The rest was a simple matter of finding the
> right gig to record, finding a mobile six-
> teen-track recording facility that didn't
> cost the moon, frantically rehearsing Grit
> and Curly Boy in not only the tunes in-
> tended for the album but enough to do the
> rest of the show as well, arranging for a
> cover photograph, trucking sound equip-
> ment all over the place, helping publicize
> the week at The Groaning Board (a live
> album requires a live audience, preferably
> a large live audience), sending out nearly a
> hundred invitations, making endless
> phone calls, driving close to two hundred
> miles a day for two weeks, and most im-
> portantly, trying to do a good show every
> night for the folks who, to our immense re-
> lief, turned out in large numbers to see the
> whole thing go down. . . . The end result of
> all this you hold in your hands, and we're
> quite pleased with it. Valerie's fingernails
> are healing nicely, thank you, and she no
> longer trembles and sweats when the word
> "album" is mentioned.

Grit Laskin has a similar recollection of the experience.
He put in a full day at his workshop, where he repaired and

handcrafted custom guitars. In the evenings, to save time, the band would meet in Grit's workshop to practise. Grit describes it this way: "We performed the same two fifty-minute sets each night. Out of those, we chose the best version of each particular song. We wound up with more material than we needed, but that suited Stan fine. He was always in the habit of recording more than he needed, just to play it safe."

The public response to *Between the Breaks* was overwhelming. The hard-core folkies, who liked Stan's traditional side, loved the album. But Stan also won over a truckload of contemporary music fans, especially in the United States. The album did what it set out to do: capture the energy of Stan Rogers live in concert. As Emily Friedman notes, this was as much due to Stan's growing awareness of his audience as it was to the live recording format.

"The energy level on *Turnaround* was down; that's what turned a lot of listeners off. The energy level on *Between the Breaks* was up, partly because it was recorded live, and partly because Stan was beginning to understand that high-energy material was selling."

In terms of song styles, *Between the Breaks* had a little bit of everything. It contained traditional songs like "Rolling Down To Old Maui" and Archie Fisher's "The Witch Of The Westmorland," and even a new version of "Barrett's Privateers" because, as Ariel reports, Stan didn't feel the original sounded "manly" enough. There were also a couple of tunes from Stan's old singer-songwriter repertoire, "First Christmas" and "Delivery Delayed."

The material Stan wrote specifically for this album was outstanding, an indication of how his songwriting skills were still developing. Of the nine tunes on the album, three were new: "Flowers Of Bermuda," "Harris And The Mare," and one that was to become his signature song, "The Mary Ellen Carter." It is from that genre peculiar to Stan Rogers, the salvage song.

> She went down last October in a
>   pouring driving rain
> The skipper, he'd been drinking and
>   the Mate, he felt no pain.
> Too close to Three Mile Rock and she
>   was dealt her mortal blow
> And the *Mary Ellen Carter* settled
>   low.

An instant classic, the song secured Stan's reputation as a songwriter and was the kind of sales-boosting "hit" *Turnaround* lacked. It is also his most inspirational song and, given the circumstances of his death, his most poignant.

> Rise again, rise again — though your
>   heart it be broken
> And life about to end
> No matter what you've lost be it a
>   home, a love, a friend
> Like the *Mary Ellen Carter*, rise
>   again.

As much as anything, "The Mary Ellen Carter" is a patented Stan Rogers political statement. He never attacked politicians or parties directly. But he often took a swipe at the unspoken relationship which underlies all politics: the relationship between the powerful and the powerless. This level of politics is evident in a previously unpublished piece giving the background to the song. It is from one of several unproduced radio plays Stan wrote, and this one was called, aptly enough, "The Mary Ellen Carter."

> Maritime insurance fraud has become big
> business, so big in fact that whole ship-

ping conglomerates have been formed in recent years whose sole purpose is not, as one would expect, the movement of goods in ship, but rather the sinking of ships in as profitable a manner as possible.

A company buys a smallish freighter, as old and rickety as possible, registers it under any of four or five "flags of convenience" like Panama, Sierra Leone, or Hong Kong, secures a cargo for a voyage, and insures the whole lot for as much as possible; usually several times the value of the ship. As soon as the ship is in deep water, it will mysteriously spring a leak and sink. The crew takes to the boats, reports the loss, and after an investigation, the insurance company pays off.

♪   ♪   ♪

On the surface, Stan seems to have simply slapped together a selection of songs for *Between the Breaks*. Like *Turnaround*, the live album played an important role in terms of Stan's career development, but it seems to lack a unifying theme. Stan used to say that the live album was "about heroes," but then, what Stan Rogers song wasn't?

If there is a theme, it is probably one of loss. In "Barrett's Privateers," the narrator has lost his legs and his youth. In "First Christmas," families are separated and lost. In "The Mary Ellen Carter," a ship is lost, as is the workers' faith in their employers, while in "White Collar Holler," the employees lose their identity. And in "The Flowers Of Bermuda" and "Harris And The Mare," what's lost is life itself. The song "Delivery Delayed" deals with what for Stan seems the most potent loss of all: the separation between the mother and her child. In this song, he describes birth from the baby's point of view.

By giant hand we're taken from the
  shelter of the womb
That dreaded first horizon, the endless empty room
Where communion is lost forever,
  when a heart first beats alone.
Still, it remembers, no matter how it
  is grown.

Stan wrote the song in 1975, to commemorate the birth of Paul Mills's son. Ariel says that in writing the song Stan became fascinated with the birth process, and, in particular, with the woman's experience of childbirth. He read books on it, asked questions, watched films in an effort to bring himself as close as possible to this experience, one which he would obviously never have.

In many ways, "Delivery Delayed" sums up Stan's inter-ests as a songwriter. He was deeply curious, and like any good Canadian songwriter, compelled by the distances between people. Perhaps this is why he returns over and over again to the theme of separation and loss: he was less interested in how far apart people were than he was in how they became sepa-rated in the first place.

To many fans, "Delivery Delayed" seems out of place on *Between the Breaks*. The song is low-key, reflective, more suited to Side Two of *Turnaround* than to the energy of a live album. But there were two good reasons for its inclusion, one of which is sacred, the other, profane.

The latter has to do with sound quality on the vinyl records. In this day of digital CDs and cassettes, physical placement of a song has no bearing on the quality of the sound produced. But on vinyl, the grooves get closer together as the record "progresses." Near the end of a side, the grooves are so tight that there isn't room for a lot of sound. That is why many albums end a side with a slow song, and that may be why *Between the Breaks* ends with "Delivery Delayed."

The sacred reason? Simple. In the second-to-last week in April, 1979, when the album was recorded, Ariel was six months pregnant. On July 16 of that year, their first and only child was born: Nathan Prescott Warren Rogers. Those were the early days of natural childbirth and Stan, a Lamaze graduate, was right there in the delivery room coaching Ariel — "Breathe, honey, dammit!" — and holding her hand. In the morning, he stood on his porch and whooped and shouted and ran down to his old van, affectionately named "Clank," and honked and honked and honked. One by one, the neighbours opened their eyes and awoke to the realization that Stan and Ariel Rogers had a son.

Stan, with hair, performing at Smale's Pace circa 1972.

Stan at sixteen with his rock band, "Stanley and the Living Stones." (Stan's the one with the glasses.)

Stan at age three, out for a paddle with his Aunt June and his grandparents (from the Bushell side) near Hazel Hill, Nova Scotia.

Stan aboard a friend's boat in Black Duck Cove, near Hazel Hill, Nova Scotia.

"The wind has blown some cold today, with just a wee touch of snow..."
Stan down in Fogarty's Cove.

An out-take from the photo shoot for the cover of *Fogarty's Cove*,
taken in Halifax in 1976.

stan rogers

I was born in Hamilton, of Nova Scotian parents, and raised on a diet of Hank Snow and Mozart. I'm a Sagittarian, with the Moon in Leo, so I'm also a hedonist, and I guess it shows in my music. I sing a lot about good times with my friends and my new family, and this imperfect but still beautiful world we all rattle around in. Most of my life has been spent around music, from the time my uncle built my first guitar out of Nova Scotia birch when I was five. One of my earliest memories of Nova Scotia is sitting around my grandmother's kitchen table with my uncles, listening to the Hank Snow, Hank Williams and Wilf Carter tunes roll out over the Moosehead beer. I had no choice, really. I had to be a musician.

I did my first paid engagement on my fourteenth birthday, at the old Ebony Knight coffee house in Hamilton. I played all night for ten dollars and a bottle of cheap wine. To this day I still loath cheap wine. But I really like entertaining people. It's an insidious disease. There's nothing like the applause to make you want to give it all back into a bigger and better show. That's something we should all remember. Everyone needs approval, and we should all be more generous with our praise of our fellow man, and more sparing with our criticism.

I've played all the coffee houses and the bars, done concerts, worked for the CBC, appeared on THE ENTERTAINERS, SHOWCASE '73, and have also done a transcription recording. I've also made records for RCA in Canada, Vanguard in the U.S.A. and now I'm under contract to a new international record company called Great Metropolitan Gramophone. But more important than any of the foregoing is my involvement with that most serene of experiences, Cedar Lake. These people are all my friends. They're all fine musicians and lovers of good music, and beautiful, warm, unique individuals to boot, and up until the time I met my old lady, the greatest highs I ever had came from sharing a stage with these folks. This is music that is vital, alive and pure Canadian. It speaks to me of the northland lakes, a painfully blue sky, and the warm sweet smell of freshly ploughed ground. It's music to share a fire with, to laugh and cry and clap your hands over, to dance to with your lady, to find some of the answers to the difficult questions of our living in.

Every man needs something in his life to fasten on to and be proud of, and Cedar Lake is lots to be proud of. Come give us a listen, and if you ever bump into me somewhere, give me a smile and let me buy you a beer, because all of this music is for you, you know.

Stan's "groovy" write-up from the Cedar Lake press kit, circa 1974.

Stan and Garnet outside Uncle Prescott's cabin at Half Way Cove,
near Canso, Nova Scotia.

Stan and Garnet, circa 1976.

The band in 1975. Left to right: Garnet, Stan, David Woodhead.

Stan believed that you were never too young to enjoy live music.
He'd often drop in at schools and give free shows.

Stan goofing off before the taping of a TV appearance in the Maritimes, circa 1975.

Stan recording *Turnaround* at Springfield Sound in London in 1977.

"No matter what you've lost . . ." Stan gives his all in a performance
of "The Mary Ellen Carter."

Stan and Ariel were married in a civil ceremony on 30 September 1977.
Left to right: Paul Mills, Garnet, Stan, Ariel, Beth McQueen, and Bev Mills.

Four generations of Rogers men, in 1981. Left to right: Nathan, Stan, Stanley, Al.

Stan at the Winnipeg Folk Festival in 1980, jamming with John Allen Cameron.

Stan's last concert, in Kerrville, Texas. The fatigue shows through.
Left to right: Garnet, Stan, Jim Morison.

Stan onstage at the Rebecca Cohn Theatre recording the live album *Home In Halifax*. He is joined here by Curly Boy Stubbs, aka Paul Mills, with Jim Morison in the background.

Stan with Nathan in 1981 at Owen Sound Folk Festival.

A family affair: Garnet, Ariel and Stan perform a Canada Day concert
at Toronto's Harbourfront, circa 1982.

"Free Stan Rogers" t-shirts were in vogue in US folk circles at a time when Stan had trouble
getting a visa to perform there. Here he's seen with Emily Friedman, editor of
"Come For To Sing," and Brit Trad folk singer Lou Killen.

A publicity shot from the Cedar Lake era.

Last Laughs

So I bid farewell to the Eastern town I never more will see.
But work I must, so eat this dust and breathe refinery
Oh, I miss the green and the woods and streams, and I don't
    like cowboy clothes
But I like being free and that makes me an idiot, I suppose.
               "The Idiot," from *Northwest Passage*

By the time of Nathan's birth, Stan had achieved such stature that he was becoming a source of humour for a lot of people. Not the laugh-behind-your-back humour of the disenfranchised or envious, but the gentle, chiding humour of peers sharing in Stan's success and at the same time warning him not to let that success inflate his already enormous ego.

Because his music was so powerful and his lyrics so appealing, Stan's songs were favourite targets of parody. The finest example is "Garnet's Home-Made Beer," a take-off on "Barrett's Privateers." Fittingly, it was written by Ian Robb, from the Friends of Fiddler's Green, who had been with Stan in Sudbury when he wrote the original. According to Robb, the parody was based on a wild party at the Rogers home, circa 1978.

"Everyone was in a funny mood, and people started throwing various liquids around. Originally it was water, but it quickly devolved into beer. My wife happened to be on the receiving end of a large jug of home-made beer, which Garnet poured over her. She was not terribly pleased."

GARNET'S HOME-MADE BEER
(to the tune of "Barrett's Privateers")

Oh, the year was 1978
(How I wish I'd never tried it now!)
When a score of men were turned
    quite green
By the scummiest ale you've ever
    seen.

CHORUS

God damn them all! I was told
This beer was worth its weight in
    gold;
We'd feel no pain, shed no tears.
But it's a foolish man who shows no
    fear
At a glass of Garnet's home-made beer

Oh, Garnet Rogers cried the town
(How I wish I'd never tried it now!)
For twenty brave men, all masochists
    who
Would taste for him his home-made
    brew

CHORUS

This motley crew was a sickening
    sight
(How I wish I'd never tried it now!)
There was caveman Dave with his
    eyes in bags;

He's a hard-boiled liver in the staggers
    and jags.

CHORUS

Well, we hadn't been there but an
    hour or two,
(How I wish I'd never tried it now!)
When a voice said: "GIMME SOME
    HOME-MADE BREW"
And Steeleye Stan hove into view.

CHORUS

Now Steeleye Stan was a frightening
    man
(How I wish I'd never tried it now!)
He was eight feet tall and four feet
    wide
Said, "Pass that jug or I'll tan your
    hide!"

CHORUS

Stan took one sip and pitched on his
    side
(How I wish I'd never tried it now!)
Garnet was smashed with a gut full of
    dregs,
And his breath set fire to both me legs.

CHORUS

So here I lay with me twenty-third beer,
(How I wish I'd never tried it now!)
It's been ten years since I felt this
    way —
On the night before my wedding day.

CHORUS

What was Stan's reaction to the song? Ian Robb and his Fiddler's Green cronies had gone to great pains to keep the song a secret — no easy task in the insular folk music community. When he finally did sing it for Stan, Robb says Stan was completely tickled and, whenever he played in Ottawa, where Robb lived, he'd drag Robb up on stage to sing the parody.

"I know what it's like to have your songs parodied," Robb says. "No one is really offended by it: a parody indicates that the song is well-loved."

♪   ♪   ♪

The biggest joke of all was played on Stan in the summer of 1980. He spent an entire month on, of all things, a school bus. He was part of a travelling folk show put together by Stan's first backer, Mitch Podolak, for Alberta's seventy-fifth anniversary celebration. The Alberta government gave Podolak $200,000 and an old bus, then let him loose.

Podolak assembled a collection of his finest musical friends: Stan Rogers, Sylvia Tyson, Connie Kaldor, the American folk singer Jim Post, John Allen Cameron, Stringband, Duck Donald's Bluegrass Band, Paul Hann and Joan MacIsaac. In all, there were forty-five people on the bus tour, including roadies, technicians and back-up musicians.

Like the other musicians on the bus trip, Joan Besen had an experience she'll never forget. Today Besen is best known for her songwriting and keyboard work with Prairie Oyster, Canada's premier country music band. In 1980, she was part of Sylvia Tyson's Great Speckled Bird. Joan recalls that the trip was an absurdity on wheels, a kind of demented high school outing for a cast of characters, the youngest of whom hadn't seen the tail end of high school in years.

"It was not a luxurious tour. You did a high-intensity show, then climbed back onto a school bus? My god! No one was twenty years old. But, while there was something

amateurish about the conditions under which we were working, there was nothing amateurish about the quality of the
shows."

Why did Stan agree to join the bus tour? For starters, the
money was good. He made close to $8,000 for thirty-three
days of work. Also, it helped Stan build on the strong support
he already had in Alberta. He often referred to Calgary as his
"second home," which put the city in contention with his
other "second homes" on the East Coast and in the United
States. Besides, Mitch was a friend, and Stan was never one
to turn his back on friends. He had a prestigious spot in the
line-up. Although Sylvia Tyson was the undisputed star, Stan
was second on the list and closed the show many nights.

"Stan definitely had one of the most powerful and moving shows you would ever see," Joan Besen recalls. "And you
could count on him, night after night." Besen knew Stan
before the tour. They'd always got along, mostly because
Besen had an instinctive understanding of how Stan ticked.

"Stan was the classic gruff-exterior-with-the-heart-of-
gold guy. He really enjoyed presenting this rough exterior. It
was kind of a test, I think, but there was also a perverse sense
of humour at work. There are certain elements in the folk
world that are very serious, very politically correct. Stan was
a big guy with a certain amount of renown and power. And it
gave him great delight to take a shot at these people whenever he could."

Mitch Podolak's biggest concern at the start of the tour
had nothing to do with logistics. He was terrified that Stan
and Jim Post would wind up killing each other. Podolak was
witness to their first meeting, at the 1978 Winnipeg Folk Festival. He introduced the two folk singers.

"Why, he's just a little guy," Stan said, without offering
his hand. "I could lift him right up and break his neck,
couldn't I?"

"You put your hand on me and I'll poke your eyes out,"
Post replied.

"Feisty too, isn't he?"

The problem was that Post intimidated Stan. The Texas

born folk singer had a great reputation as a performer and songwriter. Even though he was on the verge of stardom, Stan was still insecure at heart. But then, such insecurity is often what makes a great performer tick.

As it turned out, Podolak's worst fears never materialized. Once they got used to each other, once Stan felt he could trust Post, the two got along famously. But that's the way it often was with Stan. It took a while for Stan to feel he could trust a stranger.

While there were lots of memorable moments on the bus tour — like Post dancing naked in a field at Drummheller, just as a bus full of elderly American tourists pulled up — the highlight of the trip was the High River show. This was Joe Clark's hometown and, in 1980, its native son was prime minister.

Stan was the fourth act that night. He climbed up on stage, then strummed a chord to get the crowd's attention.

"Good evening!" he called into the mike. He stepped back and strummed another chord.

"Well, High River," he said, a twinkle in his eye. The other performers held their collective breath; they could tell Stan had something on his mind. Stan continued.

> "You've given us a prime minister . . ."
> Stan paused and smiled.
> "Better luck next time."

It was meant as a joke, but let's just say the fans didn't appreciate the humour. Stan played the rest of his show to a cold and stony silence, watching with embarrassment as audience members left in droves. The performers who followed Stan tried to win back the half empty auditorium, but their efforts were largely in vain. In a way, this was the story of Stan's life: because of his size and his talent, or maybe just because he was "a folk singer," people took him seriously all the time. This reaction confused and hurt Stan as much as his ill-fated attempts at humour confused his audience.

Delineation

Ah, for just one time, I would take the Northwest Passage
To find the hand of Franklin reaching for the Beaufort Sea
Tracing one warm line through a land so wide and savage
And make a Northwest Passage to the sea.

"Northwest Passage," from *Northwest Passage*

With *Between the Breaks*, Stan accomplished what he set out to do and then some. The album captured the feel of his live concerts and made him a hit in the American folk market.

Stan's next step was clear. Above all else, he wanted commercial success and mainstream acceptance, but on his own terms. When he first started in the music business with RCA, there was only one route to success: singles. In that kind of market, with artists vying for air time on commercial radio, Stan could never make it. But times had changed. Albums had surpassed the 45 single in importance, and album-oriented FM radio stations opened new markets. It was also possible for an artist to reach this album-buying market, without even making a dent on radio, as Stompin' Tom Connors was consistently proving.

Connors is perhaps the only other artist who can match Stan Rogers's impact in creating a contemporary identity for traditional Canadian music. The two men approached music very differently. While Stan was studied, literate and serious,

Stompin' Tom was, and remains, experienced, lyrical and light-hearted. And while Stan tried to consciously invent a Canadian folk idiom based in part on his childhood fascination with the East Coast, Connors plays and sings in the tradition of the music that surrounded him as he grew up.

Tom Connors lived the life of Stan Rogers's imagination. Born on Prince Edward Island in 1937, he was orphaned quite young, and ran away from his foster home in Skinner's Pond at the age of fourteen. Eventually, he made his way to a boarding house in St. John, New Brunswick, where he first learned to play guitar. Then he was off to work the boats.

He travelled the country coast to coast with his guitar, playing every bar and hotel lobby that would have him. In 1964, Connors found himself at the Maple Leaf Hotel in Timmins, a mining town 150 miles north of Sudbury. Soon, the crowds were streaming to the beer hall to watch a kid in black cowboy clothes sing his tunes, all the while stomping time with his boot on a piece of plywood; a perfect image of Canada. Over the next year, Connors played sold-out shows at the Maple Leaf. The owners had to expand the place three times to keep up the demand.

Connors made his first record in 1964, with his own money. Since that time he's made almost forty more. It's a staggering number given that he retired from the music business in 1978. Along the way, he started his own company, Boot Records, which in its heyday distributed sixty Canadian artists, Stan Rogers among them. Connors formed Boot Records out of sheer frustration with the Canadian music industry, having had more record company doors shut in his face than he cares to remember.

"No recording company would have anything to do with me. So I saved up my pennies by working in hotels and started making 45 singles on my own and selling them in bars. I'd go to the jukebox owners and give them 45s. Sometimes they'd put them in the jukebox; other times they'd throw them in the garbage. That's the chance you take."

Connors's tenacity paid off. Before he got fed up with the music business and retired in 1978, he had twelve gold albums

— 50,000 units of each sold — and half a dozen JUNO Awards. His albums had titles like *Bud The Spud, Stompin' Tom At The Gumboot Cloggeroo, Stompin' Tom Meets 'Muk Tuk' Annie* and *The Unpopular Stompin' Tom*, reflecting his love of home-grown stories and his less than mainstream appeal. While he might have made more money with a bigger label, Connors says he made a choice to protect the integrity of his music.

"I think that anybody who writes his own material and feels strongly about the content and subject matter is probably better off, in the beginning, with a smaller company. Stan felt strongly about his desire to represent his country through his music, and that's something a big record company just wouldn't let him get away with."

In 1990, after a twelve-year hiatus during which Connors worked on his farm and managed his other businesses, the singer returned to the public eye. The president of Capitol Records Canada, Dean Cameron, sought out the singer and persuaded him to end his self-imposed retirement.

Although he personally thought Capitol was making a big mistake, Connors relented and his first release — *Fiddle And Song* — went gold. Of the fourteen albums rereleased from Connors's back catalogue, twelve went gold — an extraordinary success story. Yet, just like Stan Rogers, Connors still doesn't get any air play outside of the CBC, and the occasional spin on a country or Maritime station.

Connors explains, "I learned very quickly that radio had no use for people who wrote songs about their own country. And I also knew that in Canada there is such a great need for people to write about this country. Everybody needs to know about their own country. This is why the music industry in the U.S. has thrived so well; they're always singing about themselves."

♪   ♪   ♪

While *Between the Breaks* was a success, Stan was frustrated with the limited scope that a single album afforded him. He wanted to incorporate the whole country in his music, something he couldn't do in ten songs. The new album *Northwest Passage* was number two in a planned five-part series, built around *Fogarty's Cove*, which would take him from one coast to the other. On this album, Stan looked at Western Canada. Others in the series would look at the Great Lakes, Quebec and Acadia (songs in French *and* English), and the Far North. Regrettably, Stan was unable to complete the last two albums in the series before he died.

Northwest Passage was recorded at London's Springfield Sound late in 1980. The album turned out to be Stan's most complete artistic achievement to date, fulfilling the promise of *Fogarty's Cove*. It has a unifying theme that goes beyond geography, with Stan once again exploring the idea of separation. Lines, especially lines of communication, are the central image of the album.

In some songs, the lines are clearly drawn. In "Northwest Passage," Stan speaks of "one warm line" of people across the snow. In "Field Behind The Plow," he talks of "straight dark rows." The hero of "Night Guard" put his "life on the line." In other songs — "Canol Road," "You Can't Stay Here" and "The Idiot" — the lines are implied.

"Lies" offers Stan's fullest contemplation of the theme. The story is of a woman, a farmer's wife, looking at her aging face in a mirror.

> She'd pass for twenty-nine, but for her
>   eyes,
> But winter lines are telling wicked lies.
> Lies!
> All those lines are telling wicked lies.

The linear quality of communications is a very Canadian concept. We see it in our routes of transportation: rivers, railway, roads and even airways, all of which are orientated along an east-west line. The irony is obvious to anyone who lives in this country: lines distance even as lines connect.

> Then she shakes off the bitter web she
>   wove,
> And turns to set the mirror, gently, face
>   down by the stove.
> She gathers up her apron in her hand.
> Pours a cup of coffee, drips Carnation
>   from the can
> And thinks ahead to Friday, 'cause Friday
>   will be fine!
> She'll look up in that weathered face that
>   loves hers, line for line,
> To see that maiden shining in his eyes
> And laugh at how the mirror tells her lies.

Stan was interested in "connections" because at that point in his life he was becoming more connected to the world around him. Parenthood, in particular, was helping Stan open up. Having understood distance, Stan was now drawn more towards connections. He was a father, after all, and Ariel says that he found being a parent both frustrating and rewarding. "He was away from home almost 300 days of the year. His children seemed like strangers at times, and Stan had a difficult time keeping up with the subtle changes in rules that go on in a home."

The demands of fatherhood had also changed since Stan's own childhood, when children were seen and not heard and fathers were the detached patriarchs of the family kingdom. By the early eighties, the pressure was on dads to be involved, sensitive and — yikes — nurturing. Like many men, Stan was ill-prepared for the job.

On the other hand, Stan truly connected with his children. Perhaps it was because he, himself, was such a child at heart. That youthful combination of insecurity and limitless faith in one's own ability was a quality Stan could appreciate.

Whatever the reasons — fatherhood, greater career and financial security, simple maturity — Stan seemed more comfortable with himself and even more focused on his career. He needed some new challenges. He had tackled Canada and criss-crossed the United States several times. Now it was time to visit the original source of his musical roots.

Letter from Scotland

Twas the same ancient fever in the Isles of the Blest
That our fathers brought with them when they "went West"
It's the blood of the Druids that never will rest
The giant will rise with the moon.

"Giant," from *Fogarty's Cove*

Carlton Hotel
Edinburgh, Scotland
25 May 1981

Ariel, Sweetheart:
I remember a time when writing letters
was one of my favourite recreations,
chiefly because, I suppose, it was a way of
easing what I conceived of to be blasted
boredom, or perhaps more likely, loneli-
ness. I also couldn't afford the phone calls
I would otherwise have had to make.
Whatever the reason, I know I spent a lot
of time at letter writing, and was told that
I wrote a good one.

More than once in the past few years,
I wondered how I fell out of the practice,
when I used to enjoy it so much. It

occurred to me this morning, that perhaps I'm not lonely anymore. Of course I miss you like crazy, but that's not the same thing at all, because I only have to look at the ring I wear to remember where I left the other half of my heart. I know that no matter where I am, I'm not really lonely anymore. So I guess letters are not as essential to my well-being as they used to be . . .

♪   ♪   ♪

The folk world had come to expect the unexpected from Stan Rogers, but no one anticipated the scope and beauty of *Northwest Passage*. Emily Friedman, in *Come For To Sing*, called the album "another brilliant and innovative record from the emerging genius of Canadian songwriting." Although the album fell short of breaking Stan into mainstream radio markets, it certainly brought him a wider audience.

Not long after *Northwest Passage* was released, Stan made his first trip to Great Britain. He was part of a ceilidh — a Gaelic word which means roughly "musical party" — sponsored in part by the International Gathering of the Clans. The feature act was Stan's old friend, guitarist and fiddler John Allen Cameron. The two had already shared the stage many times at folk festivals and clubs. Cameron even put in an appearance on the *Fogarty's Cove* album.

The idea of the ceilidh was to present the Scottish culture of Nova Scotia to the people of Scotland. A working title for the show could have been "The Coals To Newcastle Tour." Predictably, the tour was a disaster. The trouble started, Cameron recalls, as soon as the plane landed.

"We went to find our hotel, but the group in Scotland forgot we were coming. There was nothing booked, so we had to make hotel arrangements at the last minute. The next thing we found out was that there had been no promotion. We ended up filling out little hand-drawn posters ourselves, and walking all over Edinburgh, posting them."

The Canadians had two hours of singing and dancing and piping and fiddling — a great show that lacked nothing, except an audience. Over ten days, the biggest crowd to whom they played had twenty-two people in it. They finished up in a small theatre right below a punk music club.

"Stan would be doing a nice soft song, and right above us in the hall all we would hear was pounding of feet and loud drums."

Stan and John Allen decided that they owed themselves a treat. With the tour mercifully finished, they rented a car and set off to see Scotland. They headed north to Argyl where a folk festival was under way. When they arrived at the festival, they were coaxed into performing.

"We got on the stage that night, and they wouldn't let us off. Our encore was over an hour and a half. Between the songs and the fiddling and Stan's marvellous voice — he blew them away — we took the place by storm."

The two Canadians never got to sleep that night. They stayed in a pub until seven o'clock in the morning, playing, singing and swapping songs with the local musicians. Inspired by their success, the duo went out in search of more authentic Scottish music.

I managed to get a good reception in a crowed pub last night. It was straight out of a British Airways ad, decorated like the deck of a wooden sailing ship, and jammed full of people singing and laughing at the top of their lungs. I got to do a half-hour set, and they hollered for more. I had the place dead quiet at one point, too. I guess I haven't lost my touch...

John Allen Cameron is a story in himself. He was born near Mabou, in Inverness County on Cape Breton Island. It's a part of the world steeped in Celtic traditions, where fifty years ago, Gaelic was the mother tongue for many. John Allen grew up admiring the two most important people in the community: the parish priest and the local fiddler. As a teenager, John Allen entered the seminary, but dropped out before completing his vows.

John Allen eventually took a teaching degree, and wound up with a job in London, Ontario. But his first love was music, and he soon quit teaching to hang out in the folk clubs with other like-minded musicians, including an exceptional picker by the name of Paul Mills.

Thanks to his work with another Nova Scotian, Anne Murray, John Allen became an internationally known entertainer. Although he started out on fiddle, he is best known for guitar arrangements of traditional Cape Breton pipe tunes. In his heyday, John Allen thought nothing of taking his act to Las Vegas or the American talk-show circuit. For the dyed-in-the-wool folkie, these are usually acts of treason.

"I preach that music has no boundaries," Cameron says. "If it's performed well, there is no reason why traditional music can't be palatable to the unconverted. We tend to be slaves to definition, without ever really thinking things through."

Canadian music owes a debt to John Allen Cameron. He was the first performer to popularize this country's indigenous Celtic music, in particular, the music of Cape Breton Island. He forged a path that has been followed by some of Canada's best contemporary artists: Rita MacNeil, the Rankin Family, Spirit Of The West, Loreena McKennitt, the Crash Test Dummies, and, of course, Stan Rogers himself.

♪   ♪   ♪

Stan and John Allen's search for traditional Scottish music did not go well. The best they could find was a cheesy music hall revue. Later, acting on a hot tip, they wound up in a smokey folk club where a kid with ripped jeans and an acoustic guitar sang Rolling Stones and Beatles songs. Stan was displeased, to say the least. The two Canadians eventually talked their way into "Studio Two," a radio show on the BBC's Glasgow station. It was forty minutes of near chaos, songs and tremendous musicianship that left the listeners reeling, in more ways than one.

Among other things, the audience was treated to Stan singing in Gaelic and John Allen's guitar arrangements of traditional pipe tunes. They were also treated to a healthy dose of Canadian candour, courtesy Stan Rogers. It started innocently enough.

"What's your impression of our music?" the host asked.

Stan took a breath, then started up.

"The indigenous, traditional music of Scotland I love, and always have. But we've spent three nights listening to local musicians. The first night was wonderful, and the other two nights were simply..."

At this point, Stan offered the BBC's Highland Service listeners to a loud "raspberry" noise.

"They were *terrible*. We wanted to hear what highland music played by highlanders sounded like. What came out was this plastic doll dressed in a kilt that was way too short, and a jacket that was much too tight, and great knobby knees, and an English accent — or at least an anglicized Scot's accent — with a big plastic smile set on his face, doing these music hall tunes."

Not satisfied with telling the Scots how to run their own house, Stan took a swipe at the powers that be. He admonished the main sponsor of his trip — "the International Gathering of the Clowns" Stan called them — for charging Scots the equivalent of over ten dollars to see the ceilidh. He realized that he was biting the hand that fed him, but what the hell. He was on a roll, and he was never one to hide from authority.

A whole lot of things have changed in me. In a very real sense, I guess I've taken living, and making a living, very much more seriously than I ever did before. Like most of the other things I do, I overdid it. My present lousy physical condition is the end result.

I've been worried that I might not have the self-discipline I need to pull myself back into shape. But I also find that I love my life too much these days to risk screwing things up totally. In a very real sense, loving you is loving life itself, and while I suppose I should have saner reasons for wanting to lose weight and harden up my body, I really feel I want us both to live a long time together. If I make it to 83, for example, I will have loved you for sixty years. That's a pleasant thought, if ever I've had one.

love always,
Stan

Day to Day

But I long for mud under my heel
And a pocket full of pay,
So I'll take it from day to day.
"Day To Day," unreleased, from the CBC
Radio play "Famous Inside"

S tan turned the corner so quickly that no one saw the
moment coming or realized when it was past. One
instant he was just another folk singer, grunting it out
on the club and festival circuit and the next he was a star.
Sure, they still had to run their asses off. There were lots of
nights working crummy clubs, humping gear, going home
with a small percentage of the door. Even back in 1982, ten
percent of nothing was nothing. But the good gigs were getting better: auditoriums like the Rebecca Cohn Auditorium
in Halifax and the choicest spots at all the major festivals.

The biggest difference was attitude. The folk world now
acknowledged what Stan had been saying for years: he was
worth listening to. The Mariposa program said it all: "He is
considered by many the finest singer and writer Canada has
produced in decades."

What was the magic ingredient that helped Stan break
through? It might have been Jim Morison who joined the
band on bass. David Allen Eadie left after *Northwest Passage*.
Stan and Garnet were content to work without a bassist until

Morison showed up at Stan's door.

Morison met Stan the previous year during the bus tour of Alberta when Morison and his friend Bill Bourne were added to Stan's bill on the tour's last stop in Red Deer. The following spring, Stan was back in town. Someone heard that Stan was out one bass player, and urged Morison to approach him. As Morison recalls, Stan was busy that summer, but offered to give the bass player an audition in the fall if he made his own way to Hamilton.

In September, Morison arrived at Stan's door. The singer looked a little puzzled; maybe he'd forgotten his offer or maybe he figured the kid would never show. But Stan always stood by his word.

"We sat and rehearsed and drank a lot for three days. Then we went over to Garnet's place to rehearse. It didn't go over well at all. Mind you, I was extremely hung over; so was Stan. Then we drove to Ottawa to do the gig. I thought, well this is it. We'll suffer through it for two nights then I'll be sent packing."

That night on stage, however, everything clicked and the Rogers boys had a new bass player. Morison had the skill, the temperament and the size to take anything Stan and Garnet threw at him. At Garnet's age, he was bigger than Stan and that just added to the impression that the band was larger than life.

Maybe the turning point came when Stan got himself a real agent to book his engagements. Up until he met Morison, Stan had been doing all the business himself. His normal system was to start off with a patchwork schedule of appearances across the continent, then add gigs along the way. Then Stan met a young agent by the name of Jim Fleming at the Winnipeg Folk Festival. Although Fleming was fairly new to the folk music scene, he was rapidly building a reputation for his honesty, sensitivity and intelligence — a rare combination in the management side of music.

Fleming did more than just book Stan into clubs. He helped Stan form a viable plan. Fleming explains it like this: "There was something happening with Stan. His career was just growing in leaps and bounds, primarily through word of mouth. Some of it had to do with the attention he was getting on the radio, but, even then, radio wasn't that strong. Folk music wasn't getting the attention it is getting today. Stan was making it on word of mouth alone."

Whatever the reasons, Stan Rogers had turned the corner. And he was fully aware of what was happening. On a visit to Halifax months before his death, he told his Uncle Prescott that things were finally falling into place. For the first time, Prescott says, Stan could see a light at the end of the tunnel.

With Stan's rising "star" status came a new pressure: he had to live up to the billing. As a songwriter, he was a perfectionist who believed that his audience deserved no less than "the finest kind." It was already becoming tough to maintain his own high standards. As his status grew, so did his need to prove himself through his songwriting. When an artist puts this kind of pressure on himself, the result is often a creative block. And Stan was no exception. He started writing songs for his next album, tentatively called *The Great Lakes Project*, in the summer of 1981, but didn't finish until the late winter of 1983.

As Stan worked on his new album, he was also expanding his record company. In 1980, Fogarty's Cove Music added Grit Laskin's debut *Unmasked* to its list. The company was also working out the details to record *This Side Of The Ocean* by the Friends of Fiddler's Green and *La Ronde Des Voyageurs* by the Quebec group Eritage. There were also plans for a record of traditional fiddle tunes by Garnet. Things were going so well, in fact, that Stan was talking about expanding the business and had offered to sell shares to several of his friends.

Eighteen months after he started work on the Great Lakes album, Stan had enough material to record what he now called *From Fresh Water*. Paul Mills was again producer, and this time he'd helped arrange a co-production deal with the CBC. The national broadcaster would chip in with some free studio time. The deal meant that, for the first time in his recording career, Stan's songs would get the kind of care and attention that they deserved.

On The Heights

I know what it is to scale the Heights
And fall just short of fame.
But not one in ten thousand knows my name.
                              "MacDonnell On The Heights," from
                                  From Fresh Water (original lyrics)

*F*rom Fresh Water was a homecoming for Stan. It marked
the first time he had turned his artistic attention to his
true home, the province of Ontario. It was an indication
of how Stan had changed, how he could now, comfortably,
explore his own world. It was also a deliberate attempt to win
over his home province. He was well-known in the Maritimes
and the eastern United States and had pockets of support in
Alberta and along the West Coast, but at home, as the song
says, "not one in ten thousand knew his name."

Ironically, just as he was paying attention to one part of
his history, the opportunity came for him to explore another.
An organization out of the United States called Folk Tradition, dedicated to an "acoustic approach" to folk music,
commissioned Stan to do an album. The result was *For The
Family*, a selection of songs inspired by Stan's Nova Scotia
roots. For once Stan didn't write any of the lyrics. They were
all tunes he remembered from his childhood, including three
songs by his Uncle Lee Bushell and a poem by his grandfather
Sidney Bushell which Stan set to music.

For The Family was recorded on a weekend in the midst of the From Fresh Water sessions. This is how "in demand" Stan had become. And things didn't ease up when he finished his new albums. In April of 1983, as soon as From Fresh Water was in the can, the band was on the road for one of its most exhausting tours to date.

According to Jim Fleming, Stan was looking forward to a day in the not-too-distant future when he would be a big enough star to get by on just sixty live shows a year. But for now, he spent most of his days packing and unpacking his suitcase. Stan and his band started off that April on a working holiday in Bermuda, playing one of Stan's favourite venues, the Bermuda Folk Club. Then it was on to one of their coast-to-coast grinds, playing both near-empty school halls and capacity theatres. In late May, they hit the West Coast with gigs in Vancouver, Victoria, Seattle and Los Angeles. Soon, they were back at Fiddler's Green in Toronto. Then to the States to clubs like Tiger Hills and Folkway and Town Crier and Godfrey Daniel's. Next was Ottawa and the Home County Folk Festival in London, Winnipeg — for five grand — and College of St. Francis a week later for six hundred dollars. Eventually, it would seem one long blur, club after club, city after city: Grand River, Holstein's, Music Hall Golem Welcome Table RPI Ottawa Ark Bunky's Blue Whale Moorehead Duncan portalbernigoldriveredmonton — and so on, well into the new year.

But first, Kerrville, Texas.

Kerrville

He was the Captain of the *Nightingale*
Twenty-one days from Clyde in coal
He could smell the flowers of Bermuda in the gale
When he died on the North Rock Shoal.
    "The Flowers Of Bermuda," from *Between the Breaks*

Quiet Valley Ranch, Kerrville, Texas, 1 June 1983. Garnet Rogers changed his flight to leave early Tuesday morning. Stan understood. There was really no reason to stick around the Kerrville Festival. They had no more shows to play and, after two and a half months on the road, Garnet just wanted to get home to his wife Gail. In the back of his mind, Stan considered going home too; he needed a break as much as anyone. But there was still lots of gladhanding left to do, and Stan felt he had an obligation to the festival organizers to stay to the bitter end.

There was nothing on the agenda for Tuesday, except a trip to Y-O Ranch, a 40,000-acre game preserve stocked with wild animals from Africa and South America for the benefit of Texas hunters. At one point, the tour bus was attacked by a ten-foot tall ostrich which tried to peck its way through the windows. Stan laughed until his belly ached and his head turned red, all the time rooting, predictably, for the heroic bird.

That night, some of the performers went to Kerrville's only French restaurant. Connie Kaldor — who along with

Stan and Al Simmons made up the Canadian contingent at the Kerrville Festival — recalls that Stan seemed unusually reflective at dinner. "He was almost eulogizing himself. He was talking about his life and what he felt strong about and what he felt good about, and he said, how wonderful it was to have tasted success. He was basically saying 'If I die tomorrow I'll be content.' "

When Stan got back to his hotel at one o'clock in the morning, he ran into Jim Morison in the lobby. Morison was a little pissed off, having been stuck at the Holiday Inn all day with no money, while Stan was out having a good time. Stan had thought Morison had already headed home with Garnet.

Jim had a new baby boy at the time. He figured, if he was just going to sit around, he might just as well be at home. In a fit of pique, he decided to skip the closing concert and catch the next flight out.

♪   ♪   ♪

They gathered on stage for the Wednesday night grand finale. The singers linked arms and swayed in time to the music, with most of the audience — "kerrverts," as the regulars proudly called themselves — joining in. By the end of the song, everyone gathered in a big circle, half on the stage, half off, arms around shoulders, singing and swaying together, united in music.

Usually Stan loved to join in at times like this. But that night he was off to the side, alone. Perhaps he was trying to catch his breath after the long tour. In any case, he seemed deep in thought.

When the song finished, Stan perked up and headed to the hospitality trailer where he ran into Al Simmons. Without a word, Stan took out his guitar and started to sing.

> I used to love these lazy winter afternoons
> Starting out too late, giving up too
> soon . . .

Al recognized the song, Stan's "Working Joe," and realized what Stan was up to. He took out his harmonica and played along. Simmons was surprised that Stan remembered: it was a routine they'd worked up several years earlier when Stan was a guest on Al's TV show. Al's cue came when Stan reached the chorus.

> But now there's just too much to do in any
>   given day
> The car, the phone, the kiddies' shoes, too
>   many bills to pay...

Al pulled out a handkerchief and pretended to cry. He cried and cried, and finally blew his nose at which point, Stan yanked the handkerchief out of his hand. The small audience that had assembled loved the routine, thinking Al and Stan had just made it up on the spur of the moment.

The laughter and applause renewed Stan's energy. He urged Al to join him at the campfires that dotted the adjacent fields. It was a Kerrville tradition. Fans and performers got together around the firelight to share music, talk and laugh. But Al was tired and homesick, too, and decided to head off to bed.

As he watched Stan tromp off into the darkness, his guitar slung over his shoulder like a rifle, Al could see the campfires glowing in the distance and he smelled the mesquite in the air. He called out a final "goodbye" to Stan, who turned and smiled at his friend for the last time.

The Last Watch

It's the last watch on the *Midland*
The last watch alone,
The last night to love her,
The last night she's whole.
  "The Last Watch," from *From Fresh Water*

I t was a Friday night. Jim Morison was playing with his new-
born when the phone rang.
  "Have you heard?" It was Jim Fleming.
  Morison was exhausted after Kerrville, and had spent the
day sleeping and hanging out with his family. He didn't know
what Fleming was talking about.
  "Stan's plane went down in Cincinnati."
  It took a moment for Fleming's comment to sink in.
  "Did it go down soft?" Morison asked.
  "It went down hard."
  "Is everything cool? Did Stan make it?"
  Fleming didn't speak. He was searching for the words.
  "Well?"
  "No. Stan didn't make it. Turn on your TV. It's on every
station."

♪   ♪   ♪

Stan Rogers went down hard, and the folk fans who were just
getting to know and love him took his loss equally hard. They

just couldn't believe that at thirty-three he was already gone.

As often happens when a young artist suddenly dies, Stan was quickly elevated to the status of myth. The rumours started soon after the plane touched down. A woman recalled being pushed out the plane's emergency exit by a giant, bald-headed man — it could have only been Stan Rogers. The story was embellished with each retelling: two women were pushed out the exit, then three. A near-unconscious woman was carried by a giant man to the emergency exit. As she reached the bottom of the evacuation slide, she looked up to see her rescuer turn back into the fire. Soon, Stan's friends and fans were spreading the story — so widespread that it must be true — of how he valiantly carried two women, one under each massive arm, out onto the wing of the plane before diving back into the inferno, in search of more survivors.

The rumours continued. At the funeral, it is said, a statue of the Virgin Mary began to vibrate. A lone eagle soared above the gravesite and landed on the casket, just as it was about to be lowered. Since in truth there was no burial at all, it's clear that some of these rumours are the product of overactive imaginations. But one story is definitely true: Stan's twelve-string guitar, which had been previously crushed, broken, twisted and damaged on many *routine* flights, survived the fire with only minor damage.

From the ashes of Flight 797, a new figure emerged: Saint Stan. He was an extension of Rogers's Maritime Stan persona, only rougher and saltier still, with a heart of gold, a golden voice and not a spot on him. Garnet calls it the "Elvisization" of his brother. In death, we discovered Stan Rogers, bigger than ever.

Meanwhile, his family tried to pick up the pieces. Dealing with the grief and guilt and anger that accompany the sudden death of a loved one is tough enough. The existence of the record company added another dimension of difficulty. Even before Stan's death, there had been tension between Valerie and Ariel. Given the added stress of their tragedy — without Stan around to mediate — things boiled over. Stan had owned fifty-one percent of Fogarty's Cove Music Inc., while his brother owned forty-nine percent; since Stan didn't leave a will, it was up to the lawyers to decide who now owned the record company. Within the year, Ariel assumed full control of Fogarty's Cove Music, and in the fallout the family became divided: Ariel on one side and Garnet and his parents on the other. It is a rift that is only now beginning to close.

In spite of the grief and confusion, the family completed the two recording projects Stan had begun before his death. The albums were released separately, eight months apart, and stand as a testament to the remarkable range of Stan Rogers's talent.

The first album, *For The Family*, was released a few months after Stan's death. He had often referred to it as his favourite album because of the straightforward arrangements and production — guitar, bass, fiddle and vocals. Here was Stan's voice in its purest form, out in front, the way many said it should always have been recorded. Since the songs are very traditional, they tend to be less appealing to mainstream ears. But even though *For The Family* lacks any songs written by Stan himself, it offers a fascinating look at the man's musical roots and is a real treat for fans.

The second album, *From Fresh Water*, was something else entirely. It is Stan's most ambitious and personal work, a perfect blending of the traditional and singer-songwriter styles, and in terms of theme offers a prolonged meditation on triumph, achievement and attainment.

"White Squall" is a powerful start to the album, a song in which Stan's empassioned, but detached, narrative style is used to its most successful effect.

> Now it's just my luck to have the watch,
>   with nothing left to do
> But watch the deadly waters glide as we
>   roll north to the 'Soo,'
> And wonder when they'll turn again and
>   pitch us to the rail

> And whirl off one more youngster in the
>   gale.

The rest of Side One offers several glimpses of "success,"
each more personal than the last. In "The Nancy," Stan uses
a battle scene as a metaphor for the victory of substance over
style. In "Man With Blue Dolphin," Stan tells the true story
of a man out to salvage the *Bluenose's* sister ship, the *Dolphin*.
The hero's success lies in his efforts; the results, if any, are sec-
ondary. As a matter of fact, Stan might be referring to his own
career as he sings:

> And even afloat, she's a hole in the water
>   where his money goes.
> Every dollar goes
> And it's driving him crazy.

The first side ends with "Lock-keeper," which features
some of Stan's most adroit lyrics and, once again, seems a clev-
erly disguised comment on his own career.

> But that anchor chain's a fetter
> And with it you are tethered to the foam,
> And I wouldn't trade your life for one
>   hour of home.

On Side Two, Stan focuses on the destructive side of success. In "Half Of A Heart," the narrator is "fascinated by the
glitter of the flame, Watching wolves steal half of a heart
away." In "The Last Watch," an ancient lake steamer and her
old watchman find themselves callously discarded despite
years of devoted service. In "Flying," a kid unsuccessfully
attempts to make it in big league hockey. In "MacDonnell On

The Heights," a soldier finds obscurity in the face of victory:

> Twas MacDonnell raised the banner then
> And set the Heights aflame,
> But not one in ten thousand knows your
>   name.

The last song is "The House Of Orange." Although Stan once vowed never to write a political song, here it was.

> I took back my hand and showed him the
>   door.
> No dollar of mine would I part with this
>   day
> For fueling the engine of a bloody cruel
>   war
> In my forefathers' home, far away.

The voice is the exact opposite from the detached narrator who opens the album. Stan is now singing of his own heart, his own anger. Just before Stan went into the studio, a friend was badly hurt by an IRA bombing in London and Stan was understandably upset. But, while the anger in the song was genuine, Stan doesn't let it carry him away. He reshapes it until he uncovers something unique for his songs: forgiveness.

> All rights and all wrongs have long since
>   blown away,
> For causes are ashes when children lie
>   slain.
> Yet the damned U.D.L. and the cruel
>   I.R.A.

Will tomorrow go murdering again.
But no penny of mine will I add to the
     fray.
"Remember the Boyne!" they will cry out
     in vain,
For I've given my heart for the place I was
     born
And forgiven the whole House of Orange,
King Billy and the whole House of Orange.

These last two albums stand as an amazing testament to the depth and range of Stan's artistry. The albums are a tribute to a performer and songwriter who had only just approached the peak of his talents.

Rise Again

Rise again, rise again, that her name not be lost
To the knowledge of men.
      "The Mary Ellen Carter," from *Between the Breaks*

In death came the recognition that had eluded Stan all his life. He was nominated for a JUNO Award as Male Vocalist of the Year in 1984 — he eventually lost to Bryan Adams — and was presented the Diplôme d'Honneur, the highest award for artists in the country. Colin Jackson from the Canadian Council of the Arts had this to say as he presented the award.

"It is still too soon to sit down and objectively assess the impact that Stan Rogers will have on Canadian culture. But it is not too early to witness the profound effect that he had on Canadians. Like Woody Guthrie, Stan provided an articulate voice for the voiceless. The East Coast fisherman beset by Russian factory ships; the Prairie farmer, mortgage bound and tied to the land; the Great Lakes sailor surviving the storm. . . .

Those of us who had the privilege of knowing Stan and those of us who have benefitted from his writing and music are better people for it. Had he lived, Stan Rogers would have been a legend in his own time. Now he is a Canadian folk hero. Stan said it for us; Stan could inspire. . . ."

♪   ♪   ♪

Ten years after the fact, there are two perspectives on Stan's abridged career: celebration for what he achieved and regret over songs that were never written, albums that were never produced, friends that were never made, conversations that were never finished.

Today he's remembered around the world as a performer who changed the way folk music is presented, a brilliant song-writer who established a contemporary Canadian folk music genre and whose talent for the modern historic ballad has yet to be equalled. The question in everybody's mind is: *what if?* It's a question that still troubles no less then Pete Seeger, indisputably North America's greatest living folk artist. In a recent interview, Seeger told me that Stan's death was a tremendous loss, not just to Canada or to folk music, but to the world.

"He had a combination of talents that was very rare in this world: the outgoing extrovert who loved to perform on stage, but who was an extremely thoughtful man and a great songwriter. I just feel sad when I think of the hundreds of wonderful songs he would have given the world if he had lived. He was on the threshold of an extraordinary contribution."

Stan's potential was unlimited, but equally remarkable was his achievement. In his brief career, he recorded close to one hundred songs, many of which were either unreleased or released in such limited numbers that few people have heard them. Ariel is working to remedy that situation. In April, 1993, she released *Home In Halifax*, a live concert recorded by CBC one year and four months before Stan's death. It is a treasure for fans and neophytes alike, containing simple arrangements of Stan's best-known songs, some hilarious banter between Stan and Garnet and a previously unavailable gem, *Sailor's Rest*. This bittersweet song about an imaginary retirement home for seamen is destined to become a Stan Rogers classic.

No rail on the messroom table
And you're dead if you spit on the floor
There's no grog allowed, no singing too
    loud
No locks on the doors
But there's always a fire in the cardroom
And the tucker is always the best
They'll end it together
Down at the Sailor's Rest.

But Stan's legacy goes beyond the songs he recorded. Throughout his life, he struggled to change the face of Canadian music so that young artists could stay at home without sacrificing their national identity. He got the ball rolling, and in the last decade a new music industry has emerged and thrived to the point that it is the envy of many countries.

Steve Macklam is a prominent figure in this new industry. Macklam, who manages guitarist Colin James and was involved in the development of k.d. lang's career, says that Canada's music industry has become self-supporting.

"Today, a musical artist can survive in Canada. They might make a lot more money if they go down to the States, but they no longer *have* to do that in order to survive. There's a new level of comfort, which allows artists to flourish in a kind of isolation, with less concern for what's happening in other countries."

This new generation of artists — like lang, James, Blue Rodeo, Jeff Healy, Prairie Oyster, Loreena McKennitt and Rita MacNeil — sell truckloads of records in Canada and get played on every radio station, whether or not they experience any success in the U.S. And although these artists can all be considered "mainstream," they hold on to their traditional roots with a devotion that most American popular artists would never dream of.

Colin James, for example, is known as a blues guitarist, but he grew up watching folk acts like Stan Rogers, and cut his teeth playing traditional Celtic tunes on the mandolin on Canada's folk festival circuit.

It is that kind of traditional connection, according to Macklam, that is shaping Canadian music today. He says, "I think that Stan started a process that we are only beginning to see come to fruition. Whether people will attribute this to Stan Rogers, or to a deeper tradition of which he is a part, I'm not sure — but I don't think we've heard the last of him."

A deeper tradition.

That's what it was all about for Stan. He didn't just want to report history or recreate ancient musical forms, he wanted to join with that deeper tradition and become part of the musical continuum.

"I want to reflect my times," Stan once said. "I want to leave something behind that the world can look at one hundred years from now."

In the years to come, Stan's place in musical history will be a matter of discussion and argument. He couldn't have asked for more. But for now we are left with the stories and the memories and the songs of a true Canadian original. So, let the conversations end and the music begin.

Ladies and gentlemen, please put your hands together for the one, the only: Stan Rogers . . . :

> Rise again, rise again — though your
>   heart it be broken
> And life about to end
> No matter what you've lost, be it a home,
>   a love, a friend
> Like the *Mary Ellen Carter*, rise again!

Postscript

Dozens of songs, stories and poems have been written in Stan's memory. This poem is my favourite. It was written by Stan's longtime friend and frequent collaborator, Bill Howell, in June 1990.

LAMENT FOR ANOTHER DEAD FRIEND

I long to feel more; everything about this
adds up to less.
                    This is nothing but
the death of another disremembered dream.
My best memories search for what
I used to believe was compassion.
                             Abstraction,
that boat I built to navigate the numbness, sails on
without us.
                God I miss you.

And who finally cares?
The rest of the old stories pale, turn in on
themselves.
                Nothing changes them, not even
boredom or bad memory.
                        Why change anything when
it's all I can do to remember you as you were?
                               All
that heedless giving is over; some of my best friends
are becoming myths.

The hard part was learning to stop talking about
　　you behind your back.
Even to myself I started sounding as if I was
　　bragging about how well I knew you.
Praising you became a contest with your other
　　friends; the prize became the bolder noise of
　　strangers.

From piracy to privacy, nobody knew you the way
　　I did; but everybody knows you differently
　　now.
Including me.
Meanwhile even the weather has changed.
My address book is full of dead names, including
　　yours.
We always wondered
　　what would happen, but I haven't heard from
　　you for quite a while.

I wonder what it's like when you haven't had a
　　beer for seven years.
I have a beer for you, then one for me;
　　and then another for both of us.
This changes absolutely nothing that matters.
Generous to the end, our time preserves itself.
Let's drink a silent beer to that. . . .

Songs

I n his lifetime, Stan wrote more than one hundred songs. What follows is a selection featuring old favourites, big hits, unreleased rarities and some of his earliest efforts, which will be of particular interest to die-hard fans. If one of your favourite songs isn't here, don't despair; check the albums. Stan always included extensive notes, lyrics and even tuning tips in the liner notes. Each song is notated with the name of the album it comes from, if any, and a "best guess" on the year it was written.

The book *Stan Rogers: Songs From Fogarty's Cove* contains lyrics and music to the songs on Stan's first four albums. It is published by the Ottawa Folklore Centre, 744 Bronson Ave., Ottawa, Ontario, Canada, K1S 4G5.

SELECTED SONGS

Acadian Saturday Night
At Last I'm Ready For Christmas
Back In Town
Barrett's Privateers
Canol Road
Day To Day
Delivery Delayed
The Field Behind The Plow
Finch's Complaint (A Recitation)
First Christmas
Fishes
The Flowers Of Bermuda

137

Flying
Fogarty's Cove
Forty-Five Years
Free In The Harbour
Guysborough Train
Harris And The Mare
The House Of Orange
How Easy It's Become
The Idiot
The Jeannie C.
The Last Watch
Lies
Lock-keeper
MacDonnell On The Heights
Make And Break Harbour
Man With Blue Dolphin
The Mary Ellen Carter
Matter Of Heart
The Nancy
Night Guard
Northwest Passage
Once In A While
Past Fifty
Pocketful Of Gold
The Rawdon Hills
Sailor's Rest
So Blue
Song Of The Candle
Tiny Fish For Japan
Try Like The Devil
Turnaround
An Unfinished Conversation (It All Fades Away)
White Squall
Working Joe

ACADIAN SATURDAY NIGHT
Unreleased, 1974.

Uncle Emile, he's gone now nearly ten days
He "tole" his wife's he's gone for the fishing
But in the waters off St. Pierre and Miquellan Isles
The fish come in bottles of gold
If the *Anne-Marie* floats and the Mounties stay blind
He'll be back before the moon is rising
With a very fine catch all safe in the hold
Thirty cases of Trinidad light
For Acadian Saturday Night.

Emmeline Comeau works the general store
Papa says she's good for the custom
She's got eyes like fire and hair past her shoulders
As shiny black as ant'racite coal
You can see her Sunday morning on the St. Phillipe road
Her mother close behind like a dragon
But her mama don't know what she does behind the hall
Away from the music and the lights
On Acadian Saturday Night.

CHORUS

Oh — don't the fiddles make you roll
'Til your heart she pounds like a hammer
There's a fat lady beating her piano like a drum
And everybody's higher than a kite
On Acadian Saturday Night.

Granpa says it was better in his day
The Mounties stayed away from the parties
And he didn't mind a fight when the spirits got high
(You could always throw them out in the snow!)
And the rum was better and it came in bigger bottles
And the revenue cutters were slow —
Still, the old *Anne-Marie* has wings on the water
And there's nothing like Trinidad light
On Acadian Saturday Night.

CHORUS

This song almost made it onto *Turnaround*, but was dropped in favour of "The Jeannie C." Nova Scotia's Garrison Brothers do a great version of this song on their album *Thinking Of You*. "Trinidad light," by the way, is a kind of rum.

AT LAST I'M READY FOR CHRISTMAS
Unreleased, 1982.

Last Boxing Day the wife went out
The white sale for to see
In trunk load lots bought half-priced paper
And tinsel for the tree.

I packed it up for use this year
In a box I marked so plain
That stuff would sure be handy now
But it's never been seen again.

CHORUS

At last I'm ready for Christmas
I've even finished the tree
At last I'm ready for Christmas
Like I thought I'd never be.
With my feet propped up by a nice hot fire
And a matching yuletide glow
At last I'm ready for Christmas
With nearly two hours to go.

We swore this year we'd start off early
No need to rush around
The intention was to start in August
While the prices still were down.

But it was dentist this
And new bike that
And the money melts away
But I had to wait for Christmas bonus,
I did it all yesterday.

CHORUS

We must be fools, just look at that pile
You can hardly see the tree
We said this year we'd keep things simple
Then the usual spree.

But it feels so good when the kids go nuts
It's worth the toil and strain
The kids are only this young once,
and they'll never be so again.

CHORUS

This was one of Stan's last songs, written for a CBC Television Christmas Special from the National Arts Centre in Ottawa. He was in the middle of an extensive tour, and looked tired and haggard. To his embarrassment, it took him three tries to do the song without muffing the lines. The song uses the same goofy Morris dance rhythm as "The Idiot" from *Northwest Passage*.

BACK IN TOWN
Unreleased, 1982

I see him in your eyes, searching through the harbour, and out
    across the bay.
His ring is on your hand. You had a call from Cleveland
    yesterday.
Dalhousie left behind, the weather fine, he'll soon be coming
    round.

I try to hold you closer
But your Laker's back in town.

Every forty days, he leaves you there sleeping, and clears for
    Thunder Bay
You call me on the job, and cry about how long he'll be
    away.
You need a country band, a cheap hotel and me to run around
But for now it's over
Your Laker's back in town.

A distant whistle moans across the bay, pulls us apart
The singer says "We're going to slow things down."
"Your Cheating Heart" sounds like a clock run down.
Your Laker's back in town.

He comes in looking like he owns the place, and he knows
    you're here
The singer hollers "It's the final round."
The final beer feels like a rock going down
Your Laker's back in town.

The band has gone away. They're clearing off the tables, and
    giving me the eye
You took him out the door, and never thought to turn around
    and say goodbye.
And I'm the fool I know that will call and I'll be 'round
And try to hold you closer
Til your Laker's back in town.

Written for *From Fresh Water* but not included on that album, this beautiful "hurtin'" love song now exists only on a very rough demo. It is an indication of how Stan was moving into more commercial territory with his songs, without sacrificing his powerful narrative voice.

BARRETT'S PRIVATEERS
From *Fogarty's Cove*, *Between the Breaks* and *Home In Halifax*,
     1976.

Oh, the year was 1778,
(How I wish I was in Sherbrooke now!)
A letter of marque came from the King
To the scummiest vessel I've ever seen.

CHORUS

God damn them all!
I was told we'd cruise the seas for American gold
We'd fire no guns! Shed no tears!
But I'm a broken man on a Halifax pier
The last of Barrett's Privateers.

Oh, Elcid Barrett cried the town
For twenty brave men, all fishermen, who
Would make for him the *Antelope's* crew.

CHORUS

The *Antelope* sloop was a sickening sight
She'd a list to the port and her sail in rags
And the cook in the scuppers with the staggers and jags.

CHORUS

On the King's birthday we put to sea
We were ninety-one days to Montego Bay
Pumping like madmen all the way.

CHORUS

On the ninety-sixth day we sailed again
When a bloody great Yankee hove in sight
With our cracked four-pounders we made to fight.

CHORUS

The Yankee lay low down with gold
She was broad and fat and loose in stays
But to catch her took the *Antelope* two whole days.

CHORUS

Then at length we stood two cables away
Our cracked four-pounders made an awful din
But with one fat ball the Yank stove us in.

CHORUS

The *Antelope* shook and pitched on her side
Barrett was smashed like a bowl of eggs
And the main-truck carried off both me legs.

CHORUS

So here I lay in my twenty-third year
It's been six years since we sailed away
And I just made Halifax yesterday.

CHORUS

Many of the most distinguished families in Halifax made their fortunes from privateering — a form of legalized piracy. In the 1700's, the British monarchs would grant a captain "a letter of marque," a certificate that allowed the captain to attack and pillage enemy ships. In this case, the Americans were enemies of the British. Today this song is sung around the world and has been recorded dozens of times — often without proper permission, since many people do not realize that it was written in the 1970s and not the 1770s.

CANOL ROAD
From *Northwest Passage*, 1981.

Well, you could see it in his eyes as they strained against the
    night,
And the bone-white-knuckled grip upon the road.
Sixty-five miles into town, and a winter's thirst to drown
A winter still with two months left to go.
His eyes are too far open, his grin too hard and sore,
His shoulders too far high to bring relief,
But the Kopper King is hot, even if the band is not,
And it sure beats shooting whiskey-jacks and trees.

Then he laughs and says "It didn't get me this time! Not
    tonight!
I wasn't screaming when I hit the door!"
But his hands on the table top, will their shaking never stop?
Those hands sweep the bottles to the floor.
Now he's a bear in a blood-red mackinaw with hungry dogs at
    bay,
And spring-time thunder in his sudden roar.
With one wrong word he burns and the tables overturn.
When he's finished, there's a dead man on the floor.

CHORUS

Well, they'll watch for him in Carmacks, Haines and Carcross.
With Teslin blocked there's nowhere else to go.
But he hit the four-wheel drive in Johnson's Crossing;
Now he's thirty-eight miles up the Canol Road
In the Salmon Range at forty-eight below.

Well, it's God's own neon green above the mountains here
    tonight,
Throwing brittle, coloured shadows on the snow.
It's four more hours 'til dawn, and the gas is almost gone,
And that bitter Yukon wind begins to blow.

Now you can see it in his eyes as they glitter in the light,
And the bone-white rime of frost around his brow.
Too late the dawn has come; that Yukon winter's won,
And he's got his cure for cabin fever now.

CHORUS

This is the greatest cabin fever song ever written. The Kopper King Tavern really does exist, as does the Canol Road which heads north from Whitehorse to nowhere. Stan was inspired by a story he heard from a man at the Kopper King Tavern, who first caught Stan's attention when he stood on a pool table and mooned the singer.

DAY TO DAY
Unreleased, 1981.

Well it's not the hours of watch on watch
And it's not the work that I mind so much
Or the long, cold hours from my lover's touch
Though for sure she's far away.

No stranger I to the touch of steel
Or the honest fear any man can feel
But I long for mud under my heel
And a pocket full of pay,
So I'll take it from day to day.

The pack ice round us cracks and groans
The old *St. Roche* he creaks and moans
The icy fog is in my bones
And it won't go away.
Outside I bet it's warm and fair
I'd have her fingers in my hair
But it's cold wet miles to her out there
So I guess I'll have to stay,
And just take it from day to day.

We're as far north now as I want to come,
But Larson's got us under his thumb,
And I signed up for the whole damned run
I can't get off halfway.

But when I get back onto the shore
I'm going south where it stays warm
And there'll be someone on my arm
To help me spend my pay,
So I'll take it from day to day.

     This one is from the CBC Radio drama *Famous Inside*,
produced by Stan's friend Bill Howell. It is the true story of
RCMP Captain Henry Larson, who took a tiny icebreaker, the
St. Roche, through Canada's northern waters during World
War II. His purpose was to establish Canada's sovereignty
over our northern waters.

DELIVERY DELAYED
From *Between the Breaks*, 1975.

How early is "Beginning"? From when is there a soul?
Do we discover living, or, somehow, are we told?
In sudden pain, in empty cold, in blinding light of day,
We're given breath, and it takes our breath away.

How cruel to unformed fancy, the way in which we come —
Overwhelmed by feeling and sudden loss of love
And what price dark, confining pain (the hardest to forgive)
When, all at once, we're called upon to live.

By giant hand we're taken from the shelter of the womb
That dreaded first horizon, the endless empty room
Where communion is lost forever, when a heart first beats
    alone.
Still, it remembers, no matter how it's grown.

We grow but grow apart —
We live but more alone —
The more to be, the more to see,
To cry aloud that we are free
To hide our ancient fears of being alone.

And how we live in darkness, embracing spiteful cold
Refusing any answers, for no man can be told
That Delivery is delayed until we're made aware
And first reach for love, to find 'twas always there.

   Written on the occasion of the birth of Paul Mills's son,
and originally included in the "folk opera" *So Hard To Be So
Strong*. This song was also recorded by Peter, Paul and Mary,
and led Peter Yarrow of the group to call Stan "the best young
songwriter alive today."

THE FIELD BEHIND THE PLOW
From *Northwest Passage, Home In Halifax*, 1981.

Watch the field behind the plow turn to straight dark rows
Feel the trickle in your clothes. Blow the dust-cake from your
     nose.
Hear the tractor's steady roar. Oh you can't stop now;
There's a quarter section more or less to go.

And it figures that the rain keeps its own sweet time
You can watch it come for miles, but you guess you've got a
     while.
So ease the throttle out a hair. Every rod's a gain
And there's victory in every quarter mile.

CHORUS

Poor old Kuzyk down the road,
The heart-ache, hail, and hoppers brought him down
He gave it up, and went to town
And Emmett Pierce, the other day,

Took a heart attack and died at forty-two
You could see it coming on,
'Cause he worked as hard as you. . . .

In an hour, maybe more, you'll be wet clear through
The air is cooler now. Pull your hat brim further down,
And watch the field behind the plow turn to straight dark rows
Put another season's promise in the ground.

2nd CHORUS

And if the harvest's any good
The money just might cover all the loans
You've mortgaged all you own
Buy the kids a winter coat
Take the wife back East for Christmas if you can
All summer she hangs on
When you're so tied to the land.

For the good times come and go, but at least there's rain
So this won't be barren ground when September rolls around
So watch the field behind the plow turn to straight dark rows
Put another season's promise in the ground.

Very early one morning, driving across the Prairies, Stan saw a farmer working his field. That moment inspired this song, which many believe is the finest statement about the Canadian wheat farmers ever recorded.

FINCH'S COMPLAINT (A Recitation)
From *Fogarty's Cove*, 1976.

Tom Finch turned to the waitress and said:

"Bring me another Alpine. I'll have one more before I go tell Marie the news. Well boys, we're for it this time. The Plant is closed for good. Regan broke his promise, and we're through. We're working men with no work left to do.

"I always thought I'd have a boat, just like my dad before me. You don't get rich, but with boats you always could make do. But the boats gave way to trawlers, and packing turned to meal. Now that's all gone, and we're all for the dole. And the thought of that puts irons in my soul."

Tom Finch stood up and said goodbye with handshakes all around. Faces he'd grown up among, now with their eyes cast down.

Slow foot along familiar roads to the hills above the harbour. With a passing thought, "Now all this is through, and I wonder how Marie will take the news?"

The house had been so much of her, though it had hardly been a year. She'd done his father's house proud, and held it all so dear. But there was hot tea on the table when Tom came through the door. And before he spoke, she smiled and said:

"I know. The Plant is gone. Now how soon do we go?"

"We won't take a cent. They can stuff all their money. We've put a little by. And thank God there's no kids yet, or I think I'd want to die.

"We Finches have been in this part of the world for near two hundred years, but I guess it's seen the last of us. Come on, Marie, we're going to Toronto..."

Originally, "Finch's Complaint" was a song. But Stan didn't like the music, so Paul Mills suggested he try it as a recitation. In this form, it fits perfectly into the Can Trad design of *Fogarty's Cove*. "Alpine" is a brand of beer.

FIRST CHRISTMAS
From *Between the Breaks*, 1978.

This day, a year ago, he was rolling in the snow
With a younger brother in his father's yard.
Christmas break — a time for touching home
The heart of all he'd known, and leaving was so hard —
Three thousand miles away, now he's working Christmas Day
Making double time for the "minding of the store". . . .
Well, he always said he'd make it on his own,
He's spending Christmas Eve alone.
First Christmas away from home.

She's standing by the train station, panhandling for change
Four more dollars buys a decent meal and a room.
Looks like the Sally Ann place after all,
In a crowded sleeping hall that echoes like a tomb.
But it's warm and clean and free and there are worse
        places to be,
And at least it means no beating from her dad. . . .
And if she cries because it's Christmas Day
She hopes it won't show. . . .
First Christmas away from home.

In the apartment stands a tree, and it looks so small and bare
Not like it was meant to be
The Golden Angel on the top, it's not the same old silver star
You wanted for your own
First Christmas away from home.

In the morning, they get prayers, then it's crafts and tea
        downstairs
Then another meal back in his little room
Hoping maybe that "the boys" will think to phone before the
        day is gone
Well, it's best they do it soon.
When the "old girl" passed away, he fell apart more every day
Each had always kept the other pretty well

But the kids all said the nursing home was best
'Cause he couldn't live alone. . . .
First Christmas away from home.

In the Common Room they've got the biggest tree
And it's huge and cold and lifeless,
Not like it ought to be
And the lit-up Santa Claus on top
It's not the same old silver star you once made for your own
First Christmas away from home.

Stan believed that Christmas was as much a time for reflection as it was for celebration. "First Christmas" was written and first performed for a 1978 CBC Radio Christmas Special, recorded live from Sylvia Tyson's living room.

FISHES
Unreleased, 1970.

Way down in the ocean, under the shining sea
The fishes' world is in commotion,
And it's because of me.
They think the price of breathing
Is more than I can afford
But I'm living high and doing fine
Without visible means of support.

CHORUS

The fishes all think I'm dying,
Although I don't see why they care.
They're all upset because I seem to forget
That I've sometimes got to breathe air
But what care I for sun or sky,
Or things that success may bring.
The fishes all think I'm dying,
But all I want to do is sing.

Now the octopus is solicitous
He just can't see the joke
He spends his time tipping me dimes and feeding me
    so fat I choke
And the parrot fish talks as if he
Loves every word I say
He says he wants to make me rich,
But all I want to do is play.

CHORUS

Now the shark is making passes.
He thinks he'll have a bite.
He thinks he'll make a meal of me.
Well he better pull his belt up tight.
Angel fish are dancing around me in a ring
They all invite me out to play,
But all I want to do is sing.

CHORUS

    This song is a commentary on Stan's first taste of the music business. RCA wanted to turn Stan into a "novelty act," but he didn't take the bait. It's one of my favourites, maybe because it shows the humorous side that rarely made it to Stan's recordings.

THE FLOWERS OF BERMUDA
From *Between the Breaks*, 1978.

He was the Captain of the *Nightingale*
Twenty-one days from Clyde in coal
He could smell the flowers of Bermuda in the gale
When he died on the North Rock Shoal.

Just five short hours from Bermuda in a fine October gale
There came a cry "Oh, there be breakers dead ahead!"

From the collier *Nightingale*.
No sooner had the Captain brought her round, came a
     rending crash below
Hard on her beam ends, groaning, went the *Nightingale*
And overside her mainmast goes.

"Oh, Captain, are we all for drowning?" came the cry from all
     the crew.
"The boats be smashed! How are we all then to be saved?
They are stove in through and through!"

"Oh, are ye brave and hardy collier-men or are ye blind and
     cannot see?
The Captain's gig lies still before ye whole and sound;
It shall carry all o'we."

But when the crew was all assembled and the gig prepared for
     sea,
Twas seen there but eighteen places to be manned
Nineteen mortal souls were we.
But cries the Captain "Now do not delay, nor do ye spare a
     thought for me.
My duty is to save ye all now, if I can.
See ye return quick as can be."

Oh, there be flowers in Bermuda. Beauty lies on every hand,
And there be laughter, ease and drink for every man,
But there is no joy for me;
For when we reached the wretched *Nightingale* what an awful
     sight was plain
The Captain, drowned, was tangled in the mizzen-chains
Smiling bravely beneath the sea.

    Stan's favourite vacation spot was Bermuda and this song
was written with the Bermuda Folk Club in mind. Paul Mills,
who played guitar on the live album, says that this song, with
it's intricate structure, was one of the hardest he ever had to
perform.

FLYING
From *From Fresh Water*, 1982.

It was just like strapping 'em on and starting again,
Coaching these kids to the top and calling them men.
I was a third-round pick in the NHL
And that's three years of living in hell,
And going up flying, and going home dying.

My life was over the boards and playing the game,
And every day checking the papers and finding my name.
And Dad would go crazy when the scouts would call;
He'd tell me that I'd have it all
Ninety-nine of us trying, only one of us flying.

CHORUS

And every kid over the boards listens for the sound;
The roar of the crowd is their ticket for finally leaving this town.
To be just one more hopeful in the Junior A,
Dreaming of that miracle play,
And going up flying, going home dying.

I tell them to think of the play and not of the fame.
If they've got any future at all, it's not in the game.
'Cause they'll be crippled and starting all over again
Selling on commission and remembering
When they were flying, remembering dying.

CHORUS

    The true-life story of a young hockey player who got
injured before he had a chance to play in the pros. It is one of
Stan's many songs about men defeated on the verge of success.
Some fans see the last line as a chilling prophecy, contribut-
ing to the myth of Saint Stan.

FOGARTY'S COVE
From *Fogarty's Cove*, 1974.

We just lost sight of the Queensport light down the Bay before
     us
And the wind has blown some cold today
With just a wee touch of snow
Along the shore from Lazy Head, hard a-beam Half Island
Tonight we let the anchor go, down in Fogarty's Cove.

My Sally's like a raven's wing, her hair is like her mother's
With hands that make quick work of a chore
And eyes like the top of a stove
Come suppertime she'll walk the beach, wrapped in my old
     duffle
With her eyes upon the Masthead Reach, down in Fogarty's
     Cove.

CHORUS

She will walk the sandy shore so plain
Watch the combers roll in
Til I come to Wild Rose Chance again
Down in Fogarty's Cove.

She cries when I'm away to sea, nags me when I'm with her
She'd rather I'd a government job, or maybe go on the dole
But I love her wave as I put about and nose into the channel
My Sally keeps a supper and a bed for me, down in Fogarty's
     Cove.

CHORUS

     This is the song that started it all. If the chorus rhythm
sounds a little strange, it's because Stan plays around with
time. At the point where he sings "chance again," Stan
switches from common time, four beats per bar, to waltz time,
three beats per bar, then switches back again in the next bar.

The result is that the song sounds rushed for a moment, while the unusual rhythm lends the song a "real" traditional feel.

FORTY-FIVE YEARS
From *Fogarty's Cove, Home In Halifax*, 1973.

Where the earth shows its bones of wind-broken stone
And the sea and sky are one
I'm caught out of time, my blood sings with wine
And I'm running naked in the sun.
There's God in the trees, I'm weak in the knees
And the sky's a painful blue
I'd like to look around, but Honey, all I see is you.

The summer city lights will soften the night
Til you'd think that the air is clear
And I'm sitting with friends where forty-five cents
Will buy another glass of beer
He's got something to say, but I'm so far away
That I don't know who I'm talking to
Cause you just walked in the door, and Honey, all I see is you.

And I just want to hold you closer than I've ever held anyone before
You say you've been twice a wife and you're through with life
Ah, but Honey, what the hell's it for?
After twenty-three years you'd think I could find
A way to let you know somehow
That I want to see your smiling face forty-five years from now.

Alone in the lights on stage every night
I've been reaching out to find a friend
Who knows all the words, sings so she's heard
And knows how all the stories end
Maybe after the show she'll ask me to go
Home with her for a drink or two
Now her smile lights her eyes, but Honey, all I see is you.

CHORUS

A late night skinny dip formed the basis for what has become one of Stan's best-known and most recorded songs. Ariel still has the handwritten lyrics Stan sent her from Half Way Cove shortly after he wrote the song.

FREE IN THE HARBOUR
From *Northwest Passage*, 1981.

Well, it's blackfish at play in Hermitage Bay
From Pushthrough across to Bois Island.
They broach and they spout and they lift their flukes out
And they wave to a town that is dying.
Now it's many's the boats that have plied on the foam
Hauling away! Hauling away!
But there's many more fellows been leaving their homes
Where the whales make free in the harbour.

It's at Portage and Main you'll see them again
On their way to the hills of Alberta.
With lop-sided grins, they waggle their chins
And they brag of the wage they'll be earning.
Then it's quick out, pull the string, boys, and get the tool out,
Haul it away! Haul it away!
But just two years ago, you could hear the same shout
Where the whales make free in the harbour.

CHORUS

Free in the harbour.
The Blackfish are sporting again.
Free in the harbour
Untroubled by comings and goings of men
Who once did pursue them as oil from the sea,
Hauling away! Hauling away!
Now they're Calgary roughnecks from Hermitage Bay
Where the whales make free in the harbour.

Well, it's a living they've found, deep in the ground,
And if there's doubts, it's best to ignore them.
Nor think on the bones, the crosses and stones
Of their fathers that came there before them.
In the taverns of Edmonton, fishermen shout
Haul it away! Haul it away!
They left three hundred years buried up by the Bay
Where the whales make free in the harbour.

CHORUS

   This is a sequel to "Make And Break Harbour" and, for
my tastes, the superior song. While the first song was rather a
basic protest song, "Free In The Harbour" uses humour, irony
and imagery to produce a much more subtle effect. It's written in three-quarter time, "waltz" time, a rhythm Stan often
used in his songs about the sea because of the rolling, up-and-
down effect it produces. Blackfish, by the way, are small
whales.

GUYSBOROUGH TRAIN
From CBC Transcription Series Recording, out-of-print,
1972.

Now there's no train to Guysborough
Or so the man said
So it might be a good place to be.
I sit in this station
And I count up my change
And I wait for the Guysborough train.

Now I've sat in your kitchens
And talked about walls
And I've sung of your withering pain,
Shattered your temples
And I've brought on your fall
Now I wait for the Guysborough train.

CHORUS

And I ride for all time
On the Guysborough line
And I grow by the North County rain
And the North Shore's begun
The man I've become
In rags, on the Guysborough train.

No train to Guysborough
Now ain't that a shame
Though I know there will be one in time
And the house that's alone,
It soon will be gone
Razed for the Guysborough line.

CHORUS

People are simple
Like the rain clouds sweet
Both grown by that North County rain.
The Interval is clear
Will it soon disappear
Under the Guysborough train?

CHORUS

"Guysborough Train" is an early indicator of the direction Stan's songwriting would eventually take. The song had a complicated musical structure, a strong narrative voice, plus an interest in history and the Maritimes — all of which would later become Stan Rogers's trademarks.

HARRIS AND THE MARE
From *Between the Breaks*, 1979.

Harris, my old friend, good to see your face again.
More welcome, though, yon trap and that old mare,
For the wife is in the swoon, and I am all alone
Harris, fetch thy mare and take us home.

The wife and I came out for a quiet glass of stout
And a word or two with neighbours in the room
But young Cleary, he came in, as drunk and wild as sin
And swore the wife would leave the place with him.

But the wife, as quick as thought, said "No, I'll bloody not!"
And struck the brute a blow about the head
He raised his ugly paw and lashed her on the jaw
And she fell unto the floor like she were dead.

Now, Harris, well you know, I've never struck an angry blow.
Nor would I keep a friend that raised a hand
I was a "Conshie" in the war, crying "What the hell's this for?"
But I had to see his blood to be a man.

I grabbed him by his coat, spun him round and took his throat
And beat his head upon the parlour door.
He dragged out an awful knife and he roared "I'll have your
      life!"
Then he struck me and I fell unto the floor.

Blood I was from neck to thigh, bloody murder in his eye,
As he shouted out "I'll finish you for sure!"
But as the knife came down, I lashed out from the ground
And the knife was in his breast when he rolled o'er.

With the wife as cold as clay, I carried her away
No hand was raised to help us through the door
And I've brought her half a mile, but I've had to rest awhile
And none of them I'll call a friend the more.

For when the knife came down, I was helpless to the ground
No neighbour stayed his hand. I was alone
By God! I was a man, but now, I cannot stand
Now, Harris, fetch thy mare and take us home.

Oh Harris, fetch thy mare, and take us out of here
In my nine and fifty years I'd never known
That to call myself a man for my loved one I must stand
Now, Harris, fetch thy mare and take us home.

    This song started when Stan, who considered himself a pacifist, asked: "What would cause me to raise my hand at another man?" The answer was, "If they laid a hand on my wife" (although it might have easily been, "If they talk at one of my concerts"). The music is written in the key of F to accommodate Grit Laskin's Northumbrian smallpipes. In 1982, "Harris And The Mare" was adapted by the CBC for a radio play, for which Stan provided the music.

THE HOUSE OF ORANGE
From *From Fresh Water*, 1983.

I took back my hand and showed him the door.
No dollar of mine would I part with this day
For fueling the engine of a bloody cruel war
In my forefathers' home, far away,
Who fled the first famine wearing all that they owned,
Were called "Navigators," all ragged and torn,
And built the Grand Trunk here, and found a new home
Wherever their children were born.

Their sons have no politics. None can recall
Allegiance from generations before.
O'this or O'that name can't matter at all,
Or be cause enough for to war.
And meanwhile my babies are safe in their home,
Unlike their pale cousins who cower and cry

While kneecappers nail their poor dads to the floor
And teach them to hate and to die.

It's those cruel beggars who spurn the fair coin.
The peace for their kids they could take at their will.
Since the day old King Billy prevailed at the Boyne,
They've bombed and they've maimed and they've killed.
Now they cry out for money and wail at the door
But Home Rule or Republic, 'tis all of it shame;
And a curse for us here who want nothing of war.
We're kindred in nothing but name.

All rights and all wrongs have long since blown away,
For causes are ashes where children lie slain.
Yet the damned U.D.L. and the cruel I.R.A.
Will tomorrow go murdering again.
But no penny of mine will I add to the fray.
"Remember The Boyne!" they will cry out in vain,
For I've given my heart to the place I was born
And forgiven the whole House of Orange,
King Billy and the whole House of Orange.

Written in 1983, after an IRA bomb severely injured one
of Stan's friends who'd been on holiday in London. Stan wrote
this song in the studio as he neared the end of his recording
session for *From Fresh Water*. It is very likely the last song he
ever finished.

HOW EASY IT'S BECOME
Unreleased, 1975.

Last night I was taken by the words put in a play
By a young man from Three Rivers I was caught and swept
    away.
In a theatre half empty, knots of people getting cold
And wanting not to stay.

Oh, the players were a picture that could bring you to your
    feet
And they spoke of Northern beauty and the lines were so
    complete.
But applause was thin and hollow, and the writer's face was
    old,
I watched him walk away.

The empty seats all spoke of some old movie on TV
The tired past of Hollywood and Rome,
Which years away and North has brought a writer to his knees,
How easy it's become to stay at home.

In a tiny western gallery was a painter's one-man show
The first time for his children — how he'd loved to watch
    them grow.
He was proud that they were part of him, they needed to be
    sold
So he could paint again.

All the faces that he painted spoke of laughter, love and sight.
They were real enough to touch, they were strong and full of
    light
And I bought his one self-portrait, and the only one that sold.
He'll never paint again.

The crowded walls all spoke of some old movie on TV
The tired past of Hollywood and Rome,
Which years away and North has brought the painter to his
    knees,
How easy it's become to stay at home.

Another artist lost in some old movie on TV
The tired past of Hollywood and Rome,
Which years away and North has brought the painter to his
    knees,
What he could be we never would have known
How easy it's become to stay at home.

An absolute gem for Stan Rogers fans, this song was never recorded and nobody recalls Stan ever having played it. All that remains is a handwritten copy — thankfully with both words and music. He wrote it, according to his scant notes, for something called "The Great Canadian Culture Hunt." That may, however, be the song's subtitle. It's both a prophetic look at Stan's life, and an accurate picture of the plight of the artist in Canada.

THE IDIOT
From *Northwest Passage, Home In Halifax*, 1981.

I often take these night shift walks when the foreman's not
    around.
I turn my back on the cooling stacks and make for open
    ground.
Far out beyond the tank-farm fence where the gas-flair makes
    no sound
I forget the stink and I always think back to that Eastern town.

I remember back six years ago, this Western life I chose.
And every day, the new would say some factory's going to
    close.
Well, I could have stayed to take the dole, but I'm not one of
    those.
I take nothing free, and that makes me an idiot, I suppose.

So I bid farewell to the Eastern town I never more will see.
But work I must, so I eat this dust and breathe refinery.
Oh, I miss the green and the woods and streams, and I don't
    like cowboy clothes
But I like being free and that makes me an idiot, I suppose.

So come you fine young fellows who've been beaten to the
    ground.
This Western life's no paradise, but it's better than lying
    down.

Oh, the streets aren't clean, and there's nothing green, and
the hills are dirty brown,
But the government dole will rot your soul back there in your
hometown.

So bid farewell to the Eastern town you never more will see.
There's self-respect and a steady cheque in this refinery.
You will miss the green and the woods and streams, and the
dust will fill your nose.
But you'll be free, and just like me, an idiot, I suppose.

A song about Maritimers who move to Alberta to find
work is a companion piece to "Make And Break Harbour,"
also from *Northwest Passage*. "The Idiot" uses the same
"knuckle-dragging, 'neanderthal" beat as Stan's unreleased
seasonal song, "At Last I'm Ready For Christmas."

THE JEANNIE C.
From *Turnaround*, 1978.

Come all ye lads, draw near by me, that I be not forsaken
This day I lost the *Jeannie C.* and my living has been taken.

We set out this day in the bright sunrise, the same as any other
My son and I and old John Price in the boat named for my
mother.

Now it's well you know what the fishing has been — it's been
scarce and hard and cruel
But this day, by God, we sure caught cod, and we sang and
laughed like fools.

I'll never know what it was we struck, but strike we did like
thunder
John Price give a cry and pitched overside. It's forever he's
gone under.

A leak we've sprung, let there be no delay if the *Jeannie C.*
    we're saving
John Price is drown'd and slip'd away. I'll patch the hole while
    you're bailing.

But no hole I found from bow to hold. No rock it was that got
    her.
But what I found made me heart stop cold, for every seam
    poured water.

My God, I cried, as she went down. That boat was like no
    other
My father built her when I was nine, and named her for my
    mother.

And sure I could have another made in the boat shop down
    in Dover
But I would not love the keel they laid like the one the waves
    roll over.

So come all ye lads, draw near by me, that I be not forsaken
This day I lost the *Jeannie C.*, and my whole life has been taken
I'll go to sea no more.

    This song was a last-minute addition to *Turnaround*. One
of Stan's proudest moments as a songwriter came during a concert in Little Dover, not far from the "boat shop" of the song.
After he sang "The *Jeannie C.*," an old fisherman came up to
him and told Stan that the song said things that he "could
only think about" — a testament to Stan's ability to
empathize with the characters of his songs.

THE LAST WATCH
From *From Fresh Water*, 1982.

They dragged her down, dead, from Tobermory
Too cheap to spare her one last head of steam,
Deep in diesel fumes embraced,
Rust and soot upon the face of one who was so clean.

They brought me here to watch her in the boneyard,
Just two old wrecks to spend the night alone.
It's dark inside this evil place
Clouds on the moon hide her disgrace;
This whiskey hides my own.

CHORUS

It's the last watch on the Midland,
The last watch alone,
One last night to love her,
The last night she's whole.

My guess is that we were young together.
Like her's, my strength was young and hard as steel.
And like her, too, I knew my ground;
I scarcely felt the years go round
In answer to the wheel.

But then they quenched the fire beneath the boiler,
Gave me a watch, and showed me out the door.
At sixty-four, you're still the best;
One year more, and then you're less
Than the dust upon the floor.

CHORUS

So here's to useless superannuation
And us old relics of the days of steam.
In the morning, Lord, I would prefer

When the men with torches come for her,
Let the angels come for me.

CHORUS

Another story of a man — and a ship — who gets less
than his just reward. Originally titled "Midland" after a real
lake steamer, *The City Of Midland*. Paul Mills recalls that this
was one of the most difficult songs he's ever had to mix — not
for technical reasons, but because he had to put the finishing
touches on this album days after Stan's death.

LIES
From *Northwest Passage*, 1980.

At last the kids are gone now, for the day.
She reaches for the coffee as the school bus pulls away.
Another day to tend the house and plan
For Friday at the Legion, when she's dancing with her man.
Sure was a bitter winter, but Friday will be fine,
And maybe last year's Easter dress will serve her one more
    time.
She'd pass for twenty-nine, but for her eyes,
But winter lines are telling wicked lies.

CHORUS

Lies!
All those lines are telling wicked lies.
Lies, all lies!
Too many lines there in that face,
Too many to erase or to disguise —
They must be telling lies!

Is this the face that won for her the man
Whose amazed and clumsy fingers put that ring upon her
    hand?

No need to search that mirror for the years.
The menace in their message shouts across the blur of tears.
So this is Beauty's finish! Like Rodin's "Belle Heaulmiere,"
The pretty maiden trapped inside the ranch wife's toil and
        care.
Well, after seven kids, that's no surprise,
But why cannot her mirror tell her lies?

CHORUS

Then she shakes off the bitter web she wove,
And turns to set the mirror, gently, face down by the stove.
She gathers up her apron in her hand.
Pours a cup of coffee, drips Carnation from the can
And thinks ahead to Friday, 'cause Friday will be fine!

She'll look up in that weathered face that loves hers, line for
        line,
To see that maiden shining in his eyes
And laugh at how her mirror tells her lies.

CHORUS

Women were a mystery to Stan Rogers, so it's easy to see
why he considered "Lies" one of his finest artistic achievements. He spent six months working on the song. "Belle
Heaulmiere" is a sculpture which Stan describes in the
album's liner notes as "a nude of an old woman which forces
the viewer to see past the ravages of age to the young person
we all are inside."

LOCK-KEEPER
From *From Fresh Water*, 1982.

You say, "Well-met again, Lock-keeper!
We're laden even deeper than the time before,

Oriental oils and tea brought down from Singapore."
As we wait for my lock to cycle
I say, "My wife has just given me a son."
"A son!" you cry, "Is that all that you've done?"

She wears bougainvillea blossoms.
You pluck 'em from her hair and toss 'em in the tide,
Sweep her in your arms and carry her inside.
Her sighs catch on your shoulder;
Her moonlit eyes grow bold and wiser through her tears
And I say, "How could you stand to leave her for a year?"

CHORUS

"Then come with me" you say, "to where the Southern Cross
Rides high upon your shoulder."
"Come with me" you cry, "Each day you tend this lock, you're
one day older,
While your blood grows colder."
But that anchor chain's a fetter
And with it you are tethered to the foam,
And I wouldn't trade your life for one hour of home.

Sure I'm stuck here on the Seaway
While you compensate for leeway through the Trades;
And you shoot the stars to see the miles you've made.
And you laugh at hearts you've riven,
But which of these has given us more love or life,
You, your tropic maids, or me, my wife.

CHORUS

The "locks" in this song are the watery kind — although
Stan plays with the meaning. Lyrically, this is one of Stan's
most mature songs and a favourite of Tom Paxton and Paul
Mills.

MACDONNELL ON THE HEIGHTS
From *From Fresh Water*, 1982.

Too thin the line that charged the Heights
And scrambled in the clay.
Too thin the Eastern Township Scot
Who showed them all the way,
And perhaps had you not fallen,
You might be what Brock became
But not one in ten thousand knows your name.

To say the name, MacDonnell,
It would bring no bugle call
But the Redcoats stayed beside you
When they saw the General fall.
Twas MacDonnell raised the banner then
And set the Heights aflame,
But not one in ten thousand knows your name

CHORUS

You brought the field all standing with your courage and your luck
But unknown to most, you're lying there beside old General Brock.
So you know what it is to scale the Heights and fall just short of
    fame
And have not one in ten thousand know your name.

At Queenston now, the General on his tower stands alone
And there's lichen on 'MacDonnell' carved upon that
    weathered stone
In a corner of the monument to glory could you claim,
But not one in ten thousand knows your name.

CHORUS

A man named MacDonnell did fight and die alongside
General Brock in the War of 1812. But this song is as much
about another man who reached the "heights" but never

found fame: Stan himself. Stan's original lyrics read, "Not one in ten thousand knows my name." With MacDonnell, Stan found a partner in obscurity.

MAKE AND BREAK HARBOUR
From *Fogarty's Cove, Home In Halifax*, 1975.

How still lies the bay in the light Western airs
Which blow from the crimson horizon
Once more we track home with a dry, empty hold
Saving gas with the breezes so fair
She's a kindly Cape Islander, old, but still sound
But so lost in the longliner's shadow
Make and break, and maybe do, but the fish are so few
That she won't be replaced should she founder.

It's hard not to think of before the big war
When the cod went so cheap but so plenty
Foreign trawlers go by now with long-seeing eyes
Taking all, where we seldom take any
And the young folk don't stay with the fisherman's way
Long ago, they all moved to the cities
And the ones left behind, old and tired and blind
Can't work for "a pound for a penny."

CHORUS

In Make and Break Harbour the boats are so few
Too many are pulled up and rotten
Most houses stand empty. Old nets hung to dry
Are blown away, lost, and forgotten

I can see the big draggers have stirred up the bay
Leaving lobster traps smashed on the bottom
Can they think it don't pay to respect the old ways
That Make and Break men have not forgotten?
For we still keep our time to the tune of the tide

And this boat that I built with my father
Still lifts to the sky! The one-lunger and I
Still talk like old friends on the water.

     Stan completed this song and four others during a wild
weekend of writing alone in Bill Howell's house in Halifax.
The "long-seeing eyes" are the drift nets of foreign trawlers
which stretch for miles beneath the sea. Thanks to a gutless
federal government, such trawlers have destroyed the fishing
industry in Canada.

MAN WITH BLUE DOLPHIN
From *From Fresh Water*, 1982.

It was just like him. He had to pick
A boat gone from dowdy to derelict
In half a dozen years
Of searching for an owner.
She maybe left her heart in the harbour mud,
But she really caught his at the flood;
And he wonders how she knew
That she was waiting for a loner.

Blue Dolphin, built by Rhuland men,
She's lying on the bottom again
With only him to care
That *Bluenose* had a sister.
He lost the house and he sold the car
His wife walked out; so he hit the bars
And hit up every friend
To raise the *Blue Dolphin*.

CHORUS

And even afloat, she'a a hole in the water where his money goes.
Every dollar goes
And it's driving him crazy.

He pounds his fist white on the dock in the night
And cries, "I'm gonna win!"
And licks the blood away.
And he's gonna raise the Dolphin.

Blue Dolphin's lying like a wounded whale.
She's hungry for a scrap of a sail
To get her underway
Back to salt water.
Now there's a man lying spent in the winter sun.
He wonders what the hell he has done
And who would ever pay
To save his schooner daughter.

CHORUS

A Stan Rogers frustration song dressed up as a Stan Rogers salvage song. Again, it's a true story of a man who spent his life's savings raising the *Blue Dolphin*, sister ship to the *Bluenose*. Stan called the man "crazy," and from Stan that is high praise indeed.

THE MARY ELLEN CARTER
From *Between the Breaks, Home In Halifax*, 1979.

She went down last October in a pouring driving rain
The Skipper, he'd been drinking and the Mate, he felt no
  pain.
Too close to Three Mile Rock and she was dealt her mortal
  blow
And the *Mary Ellen Carter* settled low.
There was just us five aboard her when she finally was awash
We worked like hell to save her, all heedless of the cost
And the groan she gave as she went down, it caused us to
  proclaim
That the *Mary Ellen Carter* would rise again.

Well, the owners wrote her off; not a nickel would they spend.
"She gave twenty years of service, boys, then met her sorry end.
But insurance paid the loss to us, so let her rest below,"
Then they laughed at us and said we had to go.
But we talked of her all winter, some days around the clock,
For she's worth a quarter million, afloat and at the dock.
And with every jar that hit the bar we swore we would remain
And make the *Mary Ellen Carter* rise again.

CHORUS

Rise again, rise again, that her name not be lost
To the knowledge of men
Those who loved her best and were with her 'til the end
Will make the Mary Ellen Carter *rise again.*

All spring, now, we've been with her on a barge lent by a friend.
Three dives a day in a hard hat suit and twice I've had the
     bends
Thank God it's only sixty feet and the currents here are slow
Or I'd never have the strength to go below.
But we've patched her rents, stopped her vents, dogged hatch
     and porthole down
Put cables to her, 'fore and aft and girded her around
Tomorrow, noon, we hit the air and then take up the strain
And make the *Mary Ellen Carter* rise again.

CHORUS

For we couldn't leave her there, you see, to crumble into scale
She'd saved our lives so many times, living through the gale
And the laughing, drunken rats who left her to a sorry grave
They won't be laughing in another day. . . .
And you, to whom adversity has dealt the final blow
With smiling bastards lying to you everywhere you go
Turn to, and put out all your strength of arm and heart and
     brain
And, like the *Mary Ellen Carter*, rise again!

2nd CHORUS

Rise again, rise again — though your heart it be broken
And life about to end
No matter what you've lost, be it a home, a love, a friend
Like the Mary Ellen Carter, rise again.

This is Stan's signature song and considered to be one of Stan's inspirational songs. On February 12, 1983, Robert M. Cusick was on board the collier *Marine Electric* when it went down off the coast of Boston. As he lay up to his neck in the frigid water of a swamped lifeboat, fighting off hypothermia, he sang a song to keep his spirits up. The song was "The Mary Ellen Carter," and to this day, Cusick credits it with saving his life.

MATTER OF HEART
Unreleased, 1974.

We live in fear of no one to love us
Of feeling like an empty hole
No kind heart or strengthening hand
To light the dark and seeking soul.

Behind the walls of lonely protection
Afraid to give for what we may lose
And to hide our sin or let someone in
Everyone will have to choose.

CHORUS

Put your life on the line
Give your hand and pledge your time
To the love whose lips inflame you
Like some ancient and golden wine
And to all, it's a start
In fulfilling greatest needs in part

For in whatever we dream of what we someday want to be
It's a matter of heart.

We like to think we know what we're doing
We always like to be in control
The rational mind rules the passionate heart
Is what the ancient sages told
But that can sound a little bit hollow
When you're sitting by the fire alone
And the rarest of wine tastes
Of ashes and brine when
You've no one there to keep it warm.

CHORUS

The way in which our pride will stall us
When we know we should be losing control
Puts us in the fear of falling
And we let it go.
Our careful words are self-deceiving
Though we'd like to call them pretense and art
And every old bind
Is held in the mind
When it's really just a matter of heart.

CHORUS

Another song from the folk opera *So Hard To Be So Strong*. It's one of Stan's most honest songs; he was supposed to be writing about the break-up of a friend's marriage, but he may be taking a good long look at himself. The song also features one of Stan's goofiest and most charming arrangements.

THE NANCY
From *From Fresh Water*, 1982.

The clothes men wear do give them airs, the fellows to
    compare.
A colonel's regimentals shine, and women call them fair.
I am Alexander MacIntosh, a nephew to the Laird
And I do disdain men who are vain, the men with the
    powdered hair.

I command the *Nancy* schooner, from the Moy on Lake St.
    Clair.
On the third day of October, boys, I did set sail from there.
To the garrison at Amherstburg I quickly would repair
With Captain Maxwell and his wife and kids and powdered
    hair.

Aboard the *Nancy!*
In regimentals bright.
Aboard the *Nancy!*
With all his pomp and bluster there, aboard the *Nancy*-o.

Below the St. Clair rapids I sent scouts unto the shore
To ask a friendly Wyandott to say what lay before
"Amherstburg has fallen, with the same for you in store!
And militia sent to take you there, fifty horse or more."

Up spoke Captain Maxwell then, "Surrender, now, I say!
Give them your *Nancy* schooner and make off without delay!
Set me ashore, I do implore. I will not die this way!"
But says I, "You go, or get below, for I'll be on my way!"

Aboard the *Nancy!*
"Surrender, hell!" I say
Aboard the *Nancy!*
"It's back to Mackinac I'll fight, aboard the *Nancy*-o."

Well up comes Colonel Beaubien, then, who shouts as he
    comes near:
"Surrender up your schooner and I swear you've naught to
    fear.
We've got your Captain Maxwell, sir, so spare yourself his
    tears."
Says I, "I'll not but send you shot to buzz about your ears."

Well, they fired as we hove anchor, boys, and we got under
    way,
But scarce a dozen broadsides, boys, the *Nancy* did them pay
Before the business sickened them. They bravely ran away.
All sail we made, and reached the Lake before the close of day.

Aboard the *Nancy!*
We sent them shot and cheers
Aboard the *Nancy!*
We watched them running through the trees, aboard the
    Nancy-o

Oh, military gentlemen, they bluster, roar and pray.
Nine sailors and the *Nancy*, boys, made fifty run away
The powder in their hair that day was powder sent their way
By poor and ragged sailor men, who swore that they would
    stay.

Aboard the *Nancy!*
Six pence and found a day
Aboard the *Nancy!*
No uniforms for men to scorn, aboard the *Nancy*-o.

Based on a true story of a British boat during the War of
1812 that defeated an American calvary unit. Written and
performed in the style that earned Stan the nickname "Steeleye Stan," after the British revival band Steeleye Span.

NIGHT GUARD
From *Northwest Passage, Home In Halifax*, 1980.

Forty-four's no age to start again
But the bulls were getting tough and he was never free of pain
Where others blew their winnings getting tanked
Most of his got banked, saving for the farm.

He never thought she'd wait for him at all
She wanted more than broken bones and trophies on the wall
But when he quit and finally got the farm
She ran into his arms, and now they've got a kid.

CHORUS

He was star of all the rodeos but now they rob him blind
It took eighteen years of Brahma bulls and life on the line
To get this spread and a decent herd
But now he spends his time pulling Night Guard.

He told her that he'd got it for the game
A "Winnie" 303 with his initials on the frame
Riding in the scabbard at his knee. Tonight he's gonna see
Who's getting all the stock.

Seventh one this summer yesterday
Half a year of profits gone, and now there's hell to pay
The cops say they know who, but there's no proof
The banker hit the roof, and damn near took the car.

CHORUS

He hears the wire popping by the road
Sees the blacked-out Reo coming for another load
This time, it's not one they take but two
Two minutes and they're through, and laughing in the cab.

And here's the way he'll end it all
'Cause all the proof he needs is lying steady in his sights

It may be just the worst thing he could do
But he squeezes off a few, then makes his call to town.

CHORUS

A modern-day cattle rustling song, and a good example of Stan's populist politics. Stan considered this song his first serious foray into rock music. Hoping that "Night Guard" would help him reach a wider audience, he released it as the album's first single.

NORTHWEST PASSAGE
From *Northwest Passage*, 1980.

CHORUS

Ah, for just one time, I would take the Northwest Passage
To find the hand of Franklin reaching for the Beaufort Sea
Tracing one warm line through a land so wide and savage
And make a Northwest Passage to the sea.

Westward from the Davis Strait, 'tis there 'twas said to lie
The sea-route to the Orient for which so many died
Seeking gold and glory, leaving weathered broken bones
And a long-forgotten lonely cairn of stones.

Three centuries thereafter, I take passage overland
In the footsteps of brave Kelso, where his "sea of flowers" began
Watching cities rise before me, then behind me sink again
This tardiest explorer, driving hard across the plain.

CHORUS

And through the night, behind the wheel, the mileage click-
ing West

I think upon Mackenzie, David Thompson and the rest
Who cracked the mountain ramparts, and did show a path for
    me
To race the roaring Fraser to the sea.

CHORUS

How then am I so different from the first men through this
    way?
Like them I left a settled life, I threw it all away
To seek a Northwest Passage at the call of many men
To find there but the road back home again.

CHORUS

After "The Mary Ellen Carter," this is Stan's most inspirational song and a neat summary of his songwriting strategy:
to turn the ordinary into the heroic. After the album came
out, this song was featured with a stunning twelve-part harmony in the CBC Radio play *Famous Inside*. Joan Besen of
Prairie Oyster considers this one of Stan's best songs.

ONCE IN A WHILE
Unreleased, 1972.

I woke up this morning and I found that you were gone
I had to smile in knowing that it wouldn't be for long
And so I thought I'd write this song to try and make you smile
Oh, Sunday morning comes once in a while!

As if the days had speedy ways they fly on lightning wings
I dream away the noon light, and at night I only sing
And as I stand before the crowds, I have my special style
Cause Sunday morning comes once in a while!

Now if dreams were made of special days, one would fill my
    head

I'd carry with me all the things that Sunday morning said
Now I don't care how far away, I never count the miles
As long as Sunday morning comes once in a while!

CHORUS

Now I have played a hundred shows
And walked a thousand miles
And all the freaks and side men
They couldn't make me smile
And sure enough it's lonely,
Heaven only knows. . . .
Oh, Sunday morning.

I woke up this morning and I found that you were gone
I had to smile in knowing that it wouldn't be for long
And so I thought I'd write this song to try and make you smile
Oh, Sunday morning comes once in a while!

Stan Roger loved Sundays. He loved everything about the day: sleeping in, having a giant breakfast, meeting with friends and just relaxing. In fact, "Sunday" rivals "salvage" in the list of Stan's favourite subjects. His catalogue includes "Bye, Bye, Sweet Sunday," "In Your Sunday Town," "Sunday Morning," and others, some of which were not released. This particular song owes a debt to James Taylor, especially the opening line which is very similar to the opening line of Taylor's "Fire And Rain."

PAST FIFTY
From CBC Transcription Series, out-of-print, 1972.

Some living, no one time for giving,
I ain't got a dime
Wind blowin', wheatfields a growin', and none of it's mine
Got so I just watch people go by, looking my way
And I tell you I'm almost through, I'd hate to see another
    day.

CHORUS

I want to go home to the Maker
Home to the Chief
The Holy Word has made me sure my worried mind would find
    relief
I'm going through life like a pilgrim
Lost in a storm
With winds that blow to make me cold, but the Holy Body keeps
    me warm.

Lazy lady, I know you're always ready,
Selling your time
My last dollar, I pinched 'til it hollered
And bought me some wine
I'm past caring, it's all I get for sharing
So if you're for free . . .
Cause I tell you, I'm almost through
And I'm worried as a man can be.

CHORUS

Some morning like to see me warming
My feet by the fire
Eggs and bacon, coffee I'd be making
Couldn't be finer
A good living, extra bit for giving
Someone like me
And I'll tell you, I'm almost through
And I'm tired as a man can be.

CHORUS

Recorded for Stan's first CBC Transcription Series session, this song is much more upbeat than it appears on the printed page. It has a catchy melody and a strong chorus that caught the attention of Vanguard Records, who signed Stan on the basis of this potential hit. The record deal fell through and the single was never released.

POCKETFUL OF GOLD
Unreleased, 1972.

Well, the track of my beginnings
Has been buried 'neath the years
For a dozen generations,
We have toiled the land here
But now my patrimony, my inheritance is sold
To an old Rhode Island Yankee
For a pocketful of gold.

And when he comes tomorrow
I'll be giving up the land
The hills above the harbour
The rocky fields, the sand
And I'll leave my crying ocean
With shoulder to the cold
And walk out to the jingle
Of a pocketful of gold.

Inflationary Judas,
As I stare down at my hand,
For a pocketful of silver
He betrayed the Child Of Man
By me and many others, the story is retold.
How we squander our existence
For a pocketful of gold.

Now it seems like only yesterday
My heart was in the land.
From ocean unto ocean
We were true northern men.
But the invaders' smiles beguile me
And we sell all that we own
For baubles, beads and mirrors and
A pocketful of gold.

In a dozen years a new flag will be
Flying near and far

And the State of Nova Scotia will be
Just another star
And the bones of all my ancestors
Will be safe in their graves
And the beer cans and the bottles
Will be lying on the waves

Will line the shores like epitaphs:
"Our work was all in vain,"
And the Disney world of Uncle Sam
Is all that will remain.

I remember how Grandpa
Used to stare out to the sea
And raise his fist to the south
And turn and cry to me:
"Don't give up the land . . .
For a pocketful of gold."

Now the governments and the teachers tell of
Building up the land
Of how the mills and factories
Were getting out of hand
Now simple are these "Ka-nucks,"
How often I've been told,
To throw away a nation
For a pocketful of gold.

On the pocket-books of Wall Street
The old nation is a state
And of the northern mysteries
What memories remain?

I remember how Grandpa
Used to stare out to the sea
And raise his fist to the south
And turn and cry to me:
"Don't give up the land . . .
For a pocketful of gold."

Now the scenes of my childhood
Are misting in my tears
As if a veil was drawn across
The views no longer clear
My father's patrimony,
My inheritance is sold
To an old Rhode Island Yankee
For a pocketful of gold.

Stan was very anti-American at one point in his life and it particularly angered him that much of Nova Scotia was being bought up by American investors. This song has a powerful melody, but it's too long. Perhaps this is why Stan avoided "political" songs. He tended to get wrapped up in the argument and would lose sight of the song.

THE RAWDON HILLS
From *Fogarty's Cove*, 1974.

The worn down shacks of labour past on a hill of broken stone
Once brought by men to the stamping mills to crush away the
     gold
But before it could pass to their sons the glory left the hole
The Rawdon Hills once were touched by gold.

The grandsons of the mining men scratch the fields among the
     trees
When the gold played out, they were all turned out with
     granite dusted knees
But at night around the stoves, sometimes the stories still are
     told
The Rawdon Hills once were touched by gold.

Grandson of the mining men, you'll see it in your dreams
Beneath your father's bones still lies the undiscovered seam
Of quartzite in a serpentine vein that marks the greatest yield

And along the Midland Railway, it's still told
How the Rawdon Hills once were touched by gold.

Eighty years have been and gone since there was colour in the
    hole
And the careworn shades of the hard-rock men surround the
    old Cape lode
And through the tiny hillside farms the stories still unfold
The Rawdon Hills once were touched by gold.

The details are a little sketchy, but the story behind the
song goes something like this. At the turn of the century, the
Nova Scotia government circulated false reports that gold
deposits had been found in the province. The idea was to trick
people into moving to Nova Scotia. Paul Mills considers this
one of Stan's finest melodies, and the recording features a
splendid guitar solo by David Woodhead.

SAILOR'S REST
From *Home In Halifax*, 1982.

It's acrimony down in the card room
Winning hands thrown on the beize
Forgotton cards wait at the end of debate on the good old days
Captains and mates getting testy,
With memories not at their best
And tempers are flying,
Down at the Sailor's Rest.

Blue eyes in wrinkled morocco
Still search the horizon for squalls
Zeros in the sky and the watchkeeper's eye
And the pawnshop balls
The spice in the breeze out of Java
And the bars in Papeete were best
But the deck is too steady
Down at the Sailor's Rest.

Oh, how they talk of the day they'd arrive
When after the years, and the storms and the tears
Still very much alive
And oh, how the life is spilled out on the floor
In the battered old seabags, the journals and logs
And the keepsakes locked deep in the chests
That were stowed in the attic,
Down at the Sailor's Rest.

No rail on the messroom table
And you're dead if you spit on the floor
There's no grog allowed, no singing too loud
And no locks on the doors
But there's always a fire in the cardroom
And the tucker is always the best
They'll end it together
Down at the Sailor's Rest.

Oh, how they talk of the day they'd arrive
When after the years, and the storms and the tears
Still very much alive
And oh, how the life is spilled out on the floor
In the battered old seabags, the journals and logs
And the keepsakes locked deep in the chests
That were sold in the auction,
Down at the Sailor's Rest.

It's acrimony down in the card room
Winning hands thrown on the beize
Forgotten cards wait at the end of debate on the good old days
Captains and mates getting testy,
With memories not at their best
But they'll end it together
Down at the Sailor's Rest.

The only previously unreleased song on Stan's posthumous *Home In Halifax*, "Sailor's Rest" is a splendid combination of wit and sentiment. Stan wrote the song with his grandfather Stanley Rogers in mind, who was, at the time of the recording, ill in a rest home. He died shortly after the song was recorded. This is my personal favourite of all Stan's songs.

SO BLUE
From *Turnaround*, 1975.

I saw her cold in the morning light as we roared through the
 rain
Swaying softly to the ever pounding steel
Drunk upon a night of train . . . the club car's gonna take her
 again
And I'm glad to be on my own
The ocean's gonna take me home, so hungry, so alone, and so
 blue.

Somewhere back behind the darkness lies the City on the Sea
Gone already with a sleep stuck in between
I left so much behind to grow. So much, too soon, but even
 so . . .
She sways along the aisle again
Crazy woman, dancing on a train, so hungry, so alone, and so
 blue.

Cranky people do their morning jerks and the coffee bar has
 only tea
And somewhere up ahead beyond the day, there's a lady keep-
 ing warm for me
She's a mighty hand inside a silken glove
I've known it a while, and I can't get enough
I want to listen to Joni Mitchell on the radio
And make love . . .

A crazy lady on a daylight train is dancing for free
But everybody here just watches trees go by
She knows a bit of what this train can feel. Swaying spirit of
 the moving steel

She reminds me what I'm going to.
And even with the thought of you
I'm still so hungry, so alone, and so blue.
So hungry, so alone, and so blue.

This song loses a lot of its mystery when you realize that Stan wrote it on a train, the "Ocean Limited," from Halifax to Montreal. "So Blue" is Stan's tribute to one of his idols, Joni Mitchell.

SONG OF THE CANDLE
From *Turnaround*, 1972.

I took up my pen tonight. I couldn't seem to write.
It's like I got religion and then I lost the light.
An old woman once told me she'd always felt that way...
She said "Taken from the mold while it still can run
A candle might not keep you from the cold
But buy another candle, son, it's not too much to pay
For one more try." And I had to smile
Before I walked away.

Coffee houses bother me. I cannot tell you why.
But it never seems "hello" sounds as sweet as "goodbye."
And the waitresses, in passing, remember all your names...
They say "Look around and try to meet a single eye."
And "Empty cups will mock me if I stay, but
Buy another coffee, Stan, it's not too much to pay
And we will try to raise your smile
Before you walk away."

CHORUS

Tonight in a room full of candles
Another cup of ashes drains away
And at times it gets so hard to handle
Knowing one more simple song has swiftly taken wing
And I'm left alone to hear the song a lonely candle sings.

The priest, I found, was nervous. He cleared his throat a lot.
But, framed in stained glass windows, his eyes were lost in
    thought.
And I said "Father, can you tell me . . . is some happiness my
    right?"
He said "Rather seek you joy, the blessings of your God,
And Happiness from worship in His sight.
And buy another candle, son, before you start to pray
And don't forget to cross your breast
Before you walk away."

CHORUS

Tonight in a room full of candles
Another cup of madness drains away
And at times it gets so hard to handle
Knowing one more simple song has swiftly taken wing
And I'm left alone to hear the song a lonely candle sings.

One too many cigarettes, slowly burning down
And the final cup of coffee was cold and full of grounds
And maybe one last pipeful might send the words around
Still, underneath my hand this night has slipped away
And it leaves me as empty as this page
One more candle flickers out, the night is turning grey
And I just can't watch the dying flame
I have to walk away.

CHORUS

Tonight I have burned all my candles
Leaving only ashes in their wake,
And at times I get so hard to handle
Cause simple songs leave me behind, they all have taken wing
And I'm left alone to hear the song a lonely candle sings.

    An incurable romantic, Stan loved candles. At night,
he'd often read or write surrounded by a dozen of them. This
song is based on a typical subject for young writers: writers'

block. Stan's intelligent uses of metaphor and a very powerful melody save this song from adolescent self-indulgence.

TINY FISH FOR JAPAN
From *From Fresh Water*, 1982.

Where Patterson Creek's muddy waters run down
Past the penny arcades, by the harbour downtown,
All the old Turtlebacks rust in the rain
Like they never will leave there again.

But leave there they will in the hours before dawn,
Slip out in the darkness without word or song;
For a few more years yet they will work while they can
To catch tiny fish for Japan.

No white fish or trout here, we leave them alone.
The inspectors raise hell if we take any home.
What kind of fisherman can't eat his catch
Or call what he's taken his own?

But the plant runs three shifts now. There's plenty of pay.
We ship seventeen tons of garbage each day.
If we want to eat fish, then we'll open a can,
And catch tiny fish for Japan.

In the Norfolk Hotel over far too much beer,
The old guys remember when the water ran clear.
No poisons with names that we can't understand
And no tiny fish for Japan . . .

So the days run together. Each one is the same.
And it's good that the smelt have no lovelier name.
It's all just a job now, we'll work while we can,
To catch tiny fish for Japan.
And we'll catch tiny fish for Japan.

Government regulations and public tastes differ from country to country. The fishermen in this song catch smelt, which don't meet Canadian standards, and ship them to Japan, where they are a delicacy. This is another one of Stan's forgotten gems, and while many hard-core folkies object to the strings in this arrangement — strings belong in pop not folk, they say — it strikes me as a perfectly produced song. Note that "Turtlebacks" are a kind of boat.

TRY LIKE THE DEVIL
From *Turnaround*, 1975.

So it's come to the alley and playing in bars,
Coming on to the hustlers and the old burnt out stars
With the demons on my shoulders, smiling to show me the
        way.
Now there's one for ambition and another for greed
Here's a big one . . . he's a drunkard, and the easiest to feed
It takes a poor man to ignore them . . .
A rich man to drive them away.

CHORUS

No more thinking! I don't care anyway,
I can't find an answer; I've looked for one everywhere.
I'll keep my head down, and smile when they sell me
I'll play where they tell me, I'll try like the devil
To keep the demons away.

Now, it's so tantalizing, this little smell of success . . .
The monkey demon keeps me screaming, and he won't let me
        rest
Oh, someone, won't you listen, and help drive the demons
        away?

CHORUS

Written after one of Stan's few stints playing the Toronto bar scene. The band had the hardest time playing this song for the album *Turnaround*. They took numerous stabs at it, until finally, late at night, they got a take they could use. The next morning, they awoke to find the engineer had accidentally erased the song. Fed up, the band went into the studio and did the song in one take. Something must have gone right: it remains one of Stan's most soulful recordings.

TURNAROUND
From *Turnaround*, 1968.

Bits and pieces you offered of your life
I didn't think they meant a lot or said much for you
And all the chances to follow didn't make a lot of sense
When stacked up against the choices you made.

CHORUS

For yours was the open road. The bitter song,
The heavy load that I couldn't share, though the offer was there
Every time you turned around.

Now, it's not like you made out to hang around
Although . . . you know, I made some sounds to show that I
      cared.
And when it looked like you heard the call, I didn't say a lot
Although I could have said much more, had I dared.

CHORUS

And if I had followed a little ways
Because we're friends you would have made me welcome out
      there.

But we both know it's just as well, 'cause some can go
But some are meant to stay behind, and it's always that way.

2nd CHORUS

And yours is the open road. The bitter song,
The heavy load that I'll never share, though the offer was there
Every time you turned around.

This song was a last-minute addition to the album, but
made such an impression that Stan decided to make it the title
track. It was written in a style Stan hoped to sell to folk singer
Dee Higgins, who lived in Toronto at the time.

AN UNFINISHED CONVERSATION
(IT ALL FADES AWAY)
Unreleased, 1975.

An unfinished conversation,
A picture of the past
Like the one that I just found of you
Of the many that I've had
I remember I saw you laughing
With my camera close at hand
We were minutes from a quarrel
And forever from understanding.

We were just a bit excited
And a little more displeased
How you hated candid pictures
But I took them just to tease
Then you told me I was crazy
I said, "I was born that way"
And we must have said those same two lines
Twenty times a day.

CHORUS

Now I swear you don't remember why we parted
Just like I cannot remember why we loved
Ain't it funny how the past
Makes the better memories last?
Cause pain fades away,
It all fades away.

An unfinished conversation
That is somehow right within
If I just knew where to find you
Or where a letter could be sent
But I know I'm not so welcome
I know you'd nearly die
All conversations fade away
When the love light leaves the eye.

CHORUS

Written during a short hiatus in his relationship with
Ariel. She really did hate to have her picture taken, and Stan
loved to tease her by taking it. There is a very good demo
recording of this song.

WHITE SQUALL
From *From Fresh Water*, 1982.

Now it's just my luck to have the watch, with nothing left to
    do
But watch the deadly waters glide as we roll north to the 'Soo,'
And wonder when they'll turn again and pitch us to the rail
And whirl off one more youngster in the gale.

The kid was so damned eager. It was all so big and new.
You never had to tell him twice, or find him work to do.

And evenings on the mess deck he was always first to sing,
And show us pictures of the girl he'd wed in spring.

CHORUS

But I told that kid a hundred times "Don't take the Lakes for
    granted.
They go from calm to a hundred knots so fast they seem
    enchanted."
But tonight some red-eyed Wiarton girl lies staring at the wall,
And her lover's gone into a white squall.

Now it's a thing that us old-timers know. In a sultry summer
    calm
There comes a blow from nowhere, and it goes off like a bomb.
And a fifteen thousand tonner can be thrown upon her beam
While the gale takes all before it with a scream.

The kid was on the hatches, lying staring at the sky.
From where I stood I swear I could see tears fall from his eyes.
So I hadn't the heart to tell him that he should be on a line,
Even on a night so warm and fine.

CHORUS

When it struck, he sat up with a start; I roared to him, "Get
    down!"
But for all that he could hear, I could as well not made a sound.
So I clung there to the stanchions, and I felt my face go pale,
As he crawled hand over hand along the rail.

I could feel her heeling over with the fury of the blow.
I watched the rail go under then, so terrible and slow.
Then like some great dog, she shook herself and roared
    upright again.
Far overside, I heard him call my name.

CHORUS

So it's just my luck to have the watch, with nothing left to do
But watch the deadly waters glide as we roll north to the 'Soo,'
And wonder when they'll turn again and pitch us to the rail,
And whirl off one more youngster in the gale.

CHORUS

     Wiarton, a town near Owen Sound, has supplied the Great Lakes with many of her seamen. This song may be one of Stan's finest pieces of writing, but oddly enough has been overlooked by many of his fans. A production note: this song uses more guitar "parts," layers of guitar sounds recorded over top of each other, than any of Stan's other songs.

WORKING JOE
From *Northwest Passage*, 1980.

I used to love these lazy winter afternoons
Starting out too late, giving up too soon
Coming home to coffee and a "trashy" book
Never paying any mind if things were never done on time.

Time was when a fella could just let time slip away
No worries, car or telephone, just rent and food to pay
And every night with single buddies, boozing at the bar
Living for the minute, taking every hour in it.

But now there's just too much to do in any given day
The car, the phone, the kiddies' shoes, too many bills to pay
Running from the crack of dawn 'til Knowlton reads the news
And falling into bed too wiped to even kiss the wife
    goodnight.

The baby's in the Swyngomatic, singing rock and roll
My sweetie's in the kitchen, whipping up my favourite
    casserole

I knocked off work at ten o'clock, the kids are still at school
The coffee pot is perking ... to hell with bloody working.

Oh, it sure is sweet to sit at home and let time slip away
Though tomorrow I'll be scratching through another working
    day
But when I start to come apart from all the things to do
I know that I'll be taking soon another lazy winter afternoon.

Oh, just another Working Joe!

    Stan wrote this song on a "mental health day." Even
though he didn't have a regular nine-to-five, he needed a day
off every once in a while. The song just sort of wrote itself,
Ariel recalls. The baby was in the "Swyngomatic," its
methodical "click" providing Stan with the rhythm for his
song, while Ariel was nearby cooking. "Knowlton" is Knowlton Nash, long-time anchorman for the CBC's evening television newscast.

Discography

T he Canadian folk community is a tight knit group, and within it Stan Rogers built a large circle of friends — his extended family. This part of the book is dedicated to them.

What follows is an annotated discography — a list of selected recordings by Stan and other members of his folk family. Space constraints make it impossible to be comprehensive, but this list should provide a good starting point for anyone wishing to discover and listen to the folk music of Canada.

STAN ROGERS DISCOGRAPHY

As of this printing, there are seven Stan Rogers albums available. One more is forthcoming — a collection of previously unreleased songs — and, with any luck, fans may one day see a complete anthology. Stan's albums are widely available in record stores, or they can be bought directly from Fogarty's Cove Music, 23 Hillside Avenue South, Dundas, Ontario, Canada L9H 4H7. All his recordings are available in album, cassette and CD formats.

Fogarty's Cove, 1977.
Turnaround, 1978.
Between the Breaks, 1979.
Northwest Passage, 1981.
For The Family, 1983.
From Fresh Water, 1984.
Home In Halifax, 1993

TRADITIONAL MUSIC DISCOGRAPHY

This list has a slight bias towards the music of the East Coast, the traditional music that had the greatest impact on Stan Rogers. Some of these albums are available in stores, but your best bet is to contact the Canadian Society for Musical Traditions. They have an extensive catalogue of both traditional and contemporary music. All the albums on the list are available through the CSMT. Membership in the Society is very reasonable, $20 at time of writing, and entitles you to substantial discounts on all products. For more information, contact: CSMT, Box 4323, Station C, Calgary, Alberta, Canada T4T 5N1.

After The Tempest, Figgy Duff. Traditional Newfoundland songs interpreted by a great folk rock band. (Cassette, CD)

The Barley Grain For Me, Margaret Christl, Ian Robb and Grit Laskin. Traditional British songs in a Canadian context, with members of the Friends of Fiddler's Green. (LP)

Canada's Story In Song, Alan Mills. A two-album collection by one of Canada's foremost interpreters and collectors. Contains songs from various periods in Canadian history. (Cassette)

Far Canadian Fields: A Companion To The Penguin Book Of Canadian Folk Songs, various artists, compiled by Edith Fowke. The essential collection of traditional Canadian songs. (LP)

Folk Music From Nova Scotia, Various artists, from Helen Creighton's field recordings. Perhaps too academic for some, but an absolute must for anyone interested in the history of Canadian music. (Cassette)

Folk Songs Of Canada, Joyce Sullivan and Charles Jordan. The CSMT calls this the most durable of all Canadian folk albums. Once again, songs selected by Edith Fowke. (LP)

Maple Sugar: Songs of Early Canada, various artists. A two-LP collection of traditional songs, performed by contemporary artists like Stompin' Tom Connors and Harry Hibbs. (LP)

Not A Mark In This World, Anne Lederman. A scholar and performer offers a collection of her favourites — with very extensive notes. (Cassette, CD)

Songs Of The Iron Trail, Barry Luft and Tim Rogers. Traditional songs of the Canadian rails, with some great instrumental work by Grit Laskin. (Cassette, LP)

Songs Of The Newfoundland Outports, various perfomers, from Kenneth Peacock's field recordings. Another important work in the history of Canadian traditional music. (LP)

CONTEMPORARY ARTISTS DISCOGRAPHY

Most music fans are familiar with the the Big Seven of Canadian Folk: Gordon Lightfoot, Joni Mitchell, Neil Young, Leonard Cohen, Ian and Sylvia, Bruce Cockburn and Murray McLauchlan. All these artists had an effect on Stan Rogers as a songwriter and as a Canadian — and are well-known around the world. But what about other contemporary Canadian artists?

Here are fifteen albums by other Canadian folk artists. For the most part, they are Stan's contemporaries or younger artists who have followed in his footsteps and are worth a listen. I've taken a personal approach to this list: most of these artists are favourites of mine that I'd recommend to anyone, regardless of their interest in folk music.

At A High Window, Garnet Rogers.

Stan's younger brother was always recognized as a splendid musician, but he's developed into a powerful singer and songwriter — one of this country's greatest untapped talents. His earlier *Small Victories* is also recommended. Both albums contain some brilliant songwriting (the title tracks are out-

standing) and playing. *At A High Window* has the added bonus
of a tremendous back-up band that includes Colin Linden,
Dave Woodhead and Richard Bell. (Cassette, CD)

Contact: Garnet records on his own Snow Goose label.
His albums are available at record stores and through Valerie
Enterprises, c/o Woodburn Rd. RR#1, Hannon, Ontario,
Canada L0R 1P0.

A Canuck In Texas, Nigel Russell.

Stan's partner in the early days, Nigel has since moved
to Texas where he's become intrigued by the traditional musical forms of the American South. Russell is a tremendous
instrumentalist and deserves a listen by fans on both sides of
the border. (Cassette)

Contact: Calamity Records, Box 1424, Cedar Park,
Texas, USA, 78613.

A Cape Breton Classic, Carl MacKenzie.

No collection of Canadian folk music would be complete
without some Cape Breton fiddle tunes. There are a lot of
great fiddlers on the Island — the best known being Buddy
MacMaster, who has a couple albums available through
CSMT. MacKenzie, who teaches engineering at the University College of Cape Breton, is among the best. He has seven
albums to his credit, although this one is my favourite.
(Cassette)

Contact: Albums can be ordered directly from Carl,
c/o Box 5, Site 6, # 1, Sydney Forks, Nova Scotia, Canada
B0A 1W0.

Home I'll Be, Rita MacNeil.

This singer from Big Pond, Nova Scotia, offers the best
indication of what could have happened to Stan's career had
he lived. Like Rogers, MacNeil is a Canadian original, whose
music is deeply rooted in East Coast traditions, yet tempered
with an instinctive understanding of pop music. And like
Rogers, Rita MacNeil had a hard time getting record

companies to take her music seriously. Today, she is one of Canada's top selling artists, who's found a niche in both the country and western market and the adult contemporary market. *Home I'll Be* is probably her top selling album so far, and was produced by Declan O'Doherty, who was engineer on Stan's *Northwest Passage*. (Cassette, CD)

Contact: record stores.

Homeland, Bobby Watt.

A native of Scotland who now lives in Canada, Watt has a deep, rich voice, and plays contemporary music with a traditional edge. This is his debut album and it features a collection of tremendous songs and bang-on production by Garnet Rogers. (Cassette, CD)

Contact: Valerie Enterprises, CSMT.

Letters From The Coast/Sisteron, Doug McArthur.

A friend of Stan's from his London days, McArthur still tours with Garnet. Doug is a great songwriter whose work was popular in the 1970s and is on the rise again. His albums have been re-released on Garnet's Snow Goose label, and a new album is being recorded. This album is an amalgamation of two of Doug's seventies albums, remixed, which don't sound the least bit dated. *The Letters From The Coast* side is a particular favourite of mine: among its many treats is Doug's song "Hero," a minor hit for Valdy, and an early co-production credit to Danny Lanois. (Cassette)

Contact: Valerie Enterprises, CSMT.

Lila's Jig, Grit Laskin.

"The Masked Luthier Of Dupont Street" steps into the spotlight. Laskin proves that he's not just a great accompanist, as his frequent work with Stan Rogers showed, but that he can also take the spotlight. His first album *Unmasked* was released on Fogarty's Cove Music, although it's not quite as good as *Lila's Jig*. (Cassette, LP)

Contact: CSMT.

Moonlight Dancers, Bourne and MacLeod.

Guitarist, songwriter and singer Bill Bourne teams up with piper Alan MacLeod. The result is an amazing sound that takes folk well into the realms of pop, without sacrificing its integrity. The band also features Stan's last bass player Jim Morison. (Cassette, CD)

Contact: record stores, CSMT.

Oceanview Motel, Mae Moore.

This Vancouver singer-songwriter is at the forefront of a new generation of folk artists who are making an impact on both radio and TV, thanks to their videos. This album, co-produced by rocker Barney Bentall, features the hits "Red Clay Hills" and "I'll Watch Over You." (Cassette, CD)

Contact: record stores

A Proud Canadian, Stompin' Tom Connors.

A legend in Canada, Connors hasn't paid much attention to markets in other countries. Edith Fowke likens Connors to Woody Guthrie: an original working within the traditional forms of Canadian music. He's also damn funny; it's impossible to walk away from a Stompin' Tom record feeling down in the dumps. This is his "greatest hits" compilation. (Cassette, CD)

Contact: record stores.

Rose & Crown, Ian Robb.

Stan Rogers's favourite performer, Robb is a fine singer in the British tradition, a virtuoso concertina player and a good songwriter. As a member of Friends of Fiddler's Green, and on his own, Robb plays an important part in the development of both folk music and Stan Rogers's songwriting. The title song from this album is one that Stan loved and often performed in concert. (LP)

Contact: CSMT.

Save This House, Spirit Of The West.

SOTW combines traditional Celtic rhythms and forms

with high energy rock, demonstrating the continuing influence of the traditional music Stan popularized. This Vancouver-based band has been known to do a killer version of "Barrett's Privateers" in concert. (Cassette, CD)

Contact: record stores, CSMT.

Small Rebellions, James Keelaghan.

Among contemporary artists, Keelaghan is the closest to Stan Rogers in spirit. This Calgary-based musician is a powerful songwriter with a keen sense of history and identity. Keelaghan may very well be the "next big thing" on the Canadian folk music scene. (Cassette, CD, LP)

Contact: CSMT, Valerie Enterprises.

The Visit, Loreena McKennitt.

One of the greatest success stories in Canadian music history, McKennitt started off performing in the streets of Toronto and selling her home-made cassettes on the side. In a few short years, she sold more than 100,000 copies and attracted the interest of major record companies. She still records for her own Quinlan Road label, although she now has big league distribution. *The Visit* is a fascinating song-cycle, exploring Celtic musical traditions, a logical extension of the process Stan Rogers began twenty years ago. (Cassette, CD)

Contact: record stores.

The Wild Colonial Boys No. 4, The Wild Colonial Boys.

The Calgary Folk Club's house band has been around for twenty years or so. They play a mix of contemporary and traditional music, always paying close attention to their audience. This album, like all their other albums, offers a rousing good time and has the added bonus of Stan's "Field Behind The Plow." What a great name for a Canadian folk band! (Cassette, CD)

Contact: CSMT.

Index

Success without College

t our the rock & roll life from behind the scenes with Canada's intrepid and irreverent award-winning rock journalist, laurie brown, as she breaks down rock's doors and debunks a myth or two along the way. Now you can learn

⚡ TV repair in your own home

⚡ where TV meets rock & roll

⚡ why the box can't rock

⚡ why Canada rocks to a different drummer

⚡ who makes music from the head down

⚡ who makes music from the hips up

⚡ how one woman survived the world of rock TV simply by laughing

With provocative profiles of david byrne, bryan ferry, megadeth, mick jagger, kate bush, david bowie, bono and daniel lanois, among others, *Success Without College* is a dark and sweaty trip through the back alleys of rock & roll and TV.

 ISBN
0-14-016536-3

Love, Janis

*The major biography of one
of rock and roll's greatest—
and most notorious—idols.*

"Truly, this is a book for anyone who wants a
primal panorama of the culture that was the '60's,
the music that inspired it and the singer
who was Janis Joplin."
Calgary Herald

"A remarkable, no-punches-pulled view of Janis Joplin…"
Boston Globe

"Fans will welcome this intimate, poignant look at
a fondly missed superstar."
Publishers Weekly

"A thorough, restrained account of an extraordinary
rise and fall."
Kirkus Reviews

Love, Janis *is an intimate and revealing portrait of
a rock music legend, and a celebration of
a revolutionary decade.*

 0-14-017255-6

The Penguin Book of
CANADIAN FOLK SONGS
REVISED EDITION

Selected and Edited by Edith Fowke
Music Consultant: Keith MacMillan

> "I'se the b'y that builds the boat
> And I'se the b'y that sails her!
> I'se the b'y that catches the fish
> And takes 'em home to Lizer."

Folk songs are an essential part of Canadian tradition. Collected and compiled especially for Penguin, the songs in this revised volume are the direct response of Canadians—both French and English, from the earliest settlers onwards—to life in their unique country. Most of the songs date back a century or more, and in all cases the original words and tunes have been faithfully preserved. Expressive and lyrical, this original collection is a perfect introduction to the rich heritage of our native, northern land.

"*The Penguin Book of Canadian Folk Songs* is without question the most thorough, all-encompassing compilation of its kind in Canada. Its songs, all documented with a wealth of background information, represent every geographical area and every folk song type, from ballads to shanties, from love songs to broadsides and beyond. *The Penguin Book of Canadian Folk Songs* offers not only music but through that music a unique view of Canadian history."

Lois Choksy
Associate Head
Department of Music,
University of Calgary

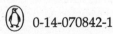 0-14-070842-1

The Penguin Encyclopedia of
POPULAR MUSIC

Edited by Donald Clarke

Rock 'n' roll. Country and western. Reggae and jazz. Folk,
gospel, and the many mutations of rhythm 'n' blues. From
Abba to ZZ Top via James Brown, Artie Shaw and Frank
Sinatra, *The Penguin Encyclopedia of Popular Music* is a criti-
cal, comprehensive, fascinating and often surprising companion to the many styles of popular music. In 1000 pages
and just over 3000 entries, this indispensable reference features performers, songwriters, musicians and record
labels—documenting the history of the business through
wars, depressions, innovations and mergers. Extensively
cross-referenced, listing the most important recordings by
each artist (in many cases, all recordings), this is the ulti-
mate resource for music lovers everywhere.

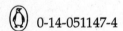 0-14-051147-4